Elizabeth Eggleston Seelye, Edward Eggleston, Charles McKew D. Parr, Ruth Parr

The Story of Columbus

Elizabeth Eggleston Seelye, Edward Eggleston, Charles McKew D. Parr, Ruth Parr

The Story of Columbus

ISBN/EAN: 9783743324541

Manufactured in Europe, USA, Canada, Australia, Japa

Cover: Foto ©ninafisch / pixelio.de

Manufactured and distributed by brebook publishing software (www.brebook.com)

Elizabeth Eggleston Seelye, Edward Eggleston, Charles McKew D. Parr, Ruth Parr

The Story of Columbus

THE
STORY OF COLUMBUS

BY
ELIZABETH EGGLESTON SEELYE

WITH NINETY-NINE ILLUSTRATIONS
BY ALLEGRA EGGLESTON

EDITED, WITH AN INTRODUCTION, BY
EDWARD EGGLESTON

NEW YORK
D. APPLETON AND COMPANY
1892

COPYRIGHT, 1892,
BY D. APPLETON AND COMPANY.

ELECTROTYPED AND PRINTED
AT THE APPLETON PRESS, U. S. A.

CONTENTS.

CHAPTER	PAGE
I.—Marco Polo	1
II.—Henry the navigator	9
III.—Young Columbus	16
IV.—Columbus in Portugal	23
V.—Columbus in Spain	30
VI.—Columbus begs in vain	35
VII.—A friendly monk	40
VIII.—Getting ready for the voyage	46
IX.—The first voyage of Columbus	51
X.—Land at last	59
XI.—Exploring in the West Indies	65
XII.—Columbus visits Cuba	70
XIII.—The discovery of Hayti	76
XIV.—Wrecked	83
XV.—A skirmish	88
XVI.—The return voyage	92
XVII.—Land	97
XVIII.—Rejoicings at court	104
XIX.—The second voyage	110
XX.—Adventures among the Caribbee Islands	116
XXI.—What had become of the colony	121
XXII.—The infant settlement and its Indian neighbors	130
XXIII.—Looking for gold	136
XXIV.—Troubles of the colony	144
XXV.—The voyage of discovery	148
XXVI.—Along the coast of Cuba	154

CONTENTS.

CHAPTER	PAGE
XXVII.—The return to Hispaniola	159
XXVIII.—What happened in the colony in the absence of Columbus	164
XXIX.—Ojeda's adventure and the war that followed	168
XXX.—Troubles for Columbus, and a new gold mine	175
XXXI.—In Spain	180
XXXII.—Columbus sets sail on his third voyage	185
XXXIII.—Columbus discovers pearls	190
XXXIV.—What happened in the colony while Columbus was away	196
XXXV.—A rebellion and a war	205
XXXVI.—Columbus and the rebels	211
XXXVII.—The king and queen displeased	218
XXXVIII.—Columbus in chains	221
XXXIX.—Columbus lands in chains	225
XL.—Columbus under a cloud	228
XLI.—Columbus predicts a hurricane	235
XLII.—Columbus at Honduras	239
XLIII.—Magic power and gold plates	245
XLIV.—Back to the land of gold	252
XLV.—Dealings with Quibian	258
XLVI.—Quibian's revenge	264
XLVII.—Stranded	269
XLVIII.—Columbus has a plan	274
XLIX.—A mutiny	278
L.—Columbus makes use of an eclipse	281
LI.—A voyage in a canoe	283
LII.—A small battle	288
LIII.—The last days of Columbus	293

LIST OF ILLUSTRATIONS.

	PAGE
Allegorical representation of Columbus as St. Christopher	Frontispiece
Gate of Pekin	1
General map of Marco Polo's journey	2
Catapult loaded. Catapult discharged	3
Passport of gold, such as the Polos used in China	4
Arrival of the Polos in Venice	5
Prince Henry the navigator	8
Position of Ceuta	9
Rock of Gibraltar	10
A ship, from an old manuscript	12
Map of the portion of the African coast discovered before Prince Henry's death	14
Gate of St. Andrea, Genoa, as it exists at present	Facing 15
Gate of St. Andrea, Genoa, as it was in the time of Columbus	15
Genoa and its harbor	16
House in which Columbus lived, as it is at present	17
Supposed appearance of the house in Columbus's time (after Staglieno)	18
Plan of the ground floor of the house in which Columbus lived (after Staglieno)	19
Cathedral of San Lorenzo, Genoa	20
Harbor of Savona	21
Portrait of Columbus	24
Map of the supposed Western Hemisphere	28
Map of Portugal, Spain, and Genoa	30

LIST OF ILLUSTRATIONS.

	PAGE
Portrait of King Ferdinand. Portrait of Queen Isabella	31
Salamanca	33
Children mocking Columbus	36
View of the Alhambra across Granada	38
With Juan Perez at the monastery	41
A window in the Alhambra	43
Gateway of Granada	44
A caravel	49
Peak of Tenerife	52
The Canary Islands and the Azores	54
Map showing the islands at which Columbus landed	60
Old print of 1500, showing Columbus landing, and the King of Spain sending ships across to America	61
A calabash	64
Indian paddling in a dug-out	66
Chair such as Columbus's messengers sat in, found in a cave on Turk's Island	74
"She may not have enjoyed the clothing very much"	78
The Indian monarch and his counsellors visit Columbus *Facing*	80
Shipwreck	83
An Indian mask from Hayti	85
An arquebus	86
A Lombard	87
Columbus finds mermaids less beautiful than they had been represented to be	89
A wampum belt	91
Columbus and the sailors draw beans	94
Columbus writes an account of his discovery	96
Shore of the Azores	98
Port of Lisbon	101
Royal palace, Barcelona	104
Seville	108
The harbor, looking from Cadiz	110
Cadiz, from the mole	107
Columbus bids good-bye to his sons *Facing*	111
Marigalante Island	113
An Indian child is found in a hut *Facing*	114
Map of Columbus's second voyage	115
The Indian trusts Columbus	123

LIST OF ILLUSTRATIONS.

	PAGE
Indian image of stone, from Santo Domingo	130
Indian figure in wood, from Santo Domingo	132
Indian figure of cotton, leather, etc., from Santo Domingo	133
Indian image of stone, from Santo Domingo	134
The Giralda Tower, Seville	137
Map of the route from Isabella to Cibao	142
Map of the voyage along the coast of Cuba	149
View of the southern shore of Hispaniola	163
Old cannon from the fortress of Santo Domingo	168
Ojeda praying to his picture of the Virgin	Facing 168
Indian battle-axe	169
Cannon of Columbus's time	170
Stone carving from Santo Domingo	172
Columbus's armor	173
Map of Hispaniola	177
Catalina tells Diaz of a new gold mine	Facing 178
South America	188
A Trinidad palm	189
Tower and fortress of Santo Domingo	196
The guana	198
Fortress and shore of Santo Domingo	200
Church of San Antonio, near Santo Domingo	201
Well at Santo Domingo, where ships get water, said to have been built by Bartholomew Columbus	206
Don Bartholomew finds his messengers dead	Facing 209
Chapel called Columbus's chapel, near Santo Domingo	211
Tower in which it is said Columbus was imprisoned	222
Interior of the fortress in which it is supposed Columbus was imprisoned	223
Portrait of Vasco da Gama, from a manuscript of his time	229
Ruins of St. Nicholas Church, Santo Domingo	231
Interior of Dominican convent, Santo Domingo	Facing 232
Ceiba tree, to which it is said the ships moored in Columbus's time	236
Map of Columbus's last voyage of discovery	240
Indian figure of stone found on the Honduras coast	243
Sea view and Indians of the Mosquito Coast	Facing 246
Characteristic Indian building on the coast	250
Don Bartholomew embraces the chief	262

LIST OF ILLUSTRATIONS.

	PAGE
Hull of a ship of Columbus's time	272
Monument to Columbus at Barcelona	291
House in Valladolid in which Columbus died	297
Cathedral of Santo Domingo, where Columbus's remains were buried	299
Palace of Santo Domingo built by Diego Columbus	302

INTRODUCTION.

BY EDWARD EGGLESTON.

THE purpose of the writer of this book has been to relate the life of the greatest of discoverers in a manner interesting and delightful to the general reader, while producing a narrative strictly conformed to the facts as given by the best ancient authorities and developed by the latest researches of scholars. There is here no attempt to discuss the pros and cons of debated points in Columbian history. Such investigators as Navarrete, Mr. Harrisse, Signor Staglieno, and our own learned Mr. Justin Winsor, have wrought abundantly and with large results upon these problems. It is the purpose of the present work to tell the story as understood through the labors of these scholars, leaving aside ponderous discussions which in a book intended for general reading would tire without enlightening.

Though disclaiming original investigation beyond the careful use of the leading authorities, Mrs. Seelye has been at much pains not to give the reader the discredited myths used by the old school of biographers.

It is a poor service to relate as history an interesting story that is not true, or to lift an historical figure into a heroism far from his real character. To give the facts as we know them, and to show Columbus as he really was, has been the sincere endeavor of the writer of this book. The story is wonderful enough without the embellishment of fiction; the man is interesting enough when painted in his real colors.

The curious researches of Mr. Henry Harrisse into the personal life of Columbus, the results of which have been given to the world in monographs in several languages, have assisted the author to give it a personal coloring which is always a legitimate source of interest, especially to the young reader. One can hardly speak too highly of the patient ingenuity by which the antiquary Signor Staglieno has managed to find and identify beyond doubt the house in which Columbus lived as a boy. Such investigations dissipate error, and make us know the real man and his environment.

It was the fashion of the older modern biographers of Columbus, of whom Irving was the chief, to see all the Christian virtues in their subject. The school of romantic history and biography was as characteristic of the first half of the present century as the school of romantic fiction and poetry. Both sought at all costs to find a hero, and, whenever possible, to set over against this central figure a heroine. When the discovery of America was the theme, Columbus became a knight-errant with an admixture of saintliness, while Isabella played the counterpart of heroine, to maintain the symmetry of the narrative. Such a method belonged to a poetic age and had its uses, but it was fatal to sound historical conclusions. It reached its extreme of folly in the movement set on foot to have Columbus canonized by the Church for a saint.

We have now swung to another extreme in our literary methods. Producing fiction much of which is quite too sordid to be justly called realistic, we are possessed at the same time with a sort of rage to debase the great figures of history. Not content with robbing them of the false laurels with which our imaginative predecessors have crowned them, we give way to a pessimistic passion for denying them any virtue at all. Because they have been praised for qualities they have not, we scorn them for false pretenders. One of the worst sufferers from this reaction is the great Genoese sailor whose achievement of four hundred years ago gave to civilization a world unknown before. There seems to be an emulation of detraction among the most recent investigators and learned biographers. To paint the discoverer in the darkest colors is accounted nowadays an evidence of scholarship. But the pessimistic and destructive mode of judgment is as far from being scientific as the now discarded romantic treatment, while it is much less agreeable. Historic justice remembers the wisdom expressed in the motto which was Lord Bacon's device, and settles itself in a secure moderation.

Let us grant, then, that this great navigator was not a saint. Like other great men, he had faults even when judged by the light of his own time; and we have no right to censure him by the standards of our age. But he was a great fifteenth-century man. He could hardly have won his battle had he not had some of the faults of his age. He has been blamed for not having the qualities of Copernicus or Las Casas. We must not expect too much for our shilling. Columbus had in a degree rarely equaled the power to consecrate himself to one great achievement. He had courage, fortitude, and a mastery of navigation as then understood. In a word, he only had all that was needed to produce a man capable of crossing the Sea of Darkness. No other navigator of his time had conceptions so bold or a pertinacity of pursuit so unflagging. Men of aptitudes so special are usually one-sided. History will not lay it up against General Grant that he was a weak statesman, nor will posterity insist on remembering that Turner, the painter, wrote bad poetry. It is enough that Columbus alone of the men of the fifteenth century had the imagination to plan and the boldness to carry out a voyage in search of land to the westward. No one can make him less than what his own merit has made him, the most conspicuous figure in the history of his age—the man who rendered the world the greatest service possible at that moment.

He was not in advance of his age in other respects. He was superstitious; he was ambitious; he sought wealth, which was the prize that spurred other Genoese adventurers to hard tasks. He lacked the enthusiasm of disinterested research which possessed Copernicus and the reformatory spirit of Las Casas. But neither Copernicus nor Las Casas ever dreamed of setting out to find land by the untried water way to the westward, nor could either of them have set on foot so bold an undertaking. Nature does not give everything to one man. And the very faults charged against Columbus—his pursuit of wealth and his belief in his own divine mission—propelled and supported him in his arduous and perilous enterprise. Let us judge him fairly and by the standards of his age, and honor him for what he was and did, without censuring him that he was not something else. To rob the doers of great deeds of their hard-earned glory, is to deprive the race of one of the mainsprings of notable actions.

In the laborious task of gathering material for authentic pictures, the illustrator has been placed under obligation by the kindness of several gentlemen. Mr. Nathan Appleton, of Boston, generously put at her disposal a valuable collection of photographs, and several drawings made under his own supervision in the island of Santo Domingo. Mr. E. C. Perry, of Honduras, also placed his collection in her hands. Acknowledgments are also due to Mr. Henry Marquand, of New York, Prof. Otis T. Mason, of the National Museum, and to others.

It remains only to say that the present book is the first of a series intended to introduce the young reader and the general reader to what is most interesting and delightful in American history. It is the result of the co-operation of two sisters already known to the public by work in their several departments. I have taken a lively interest in this labor of my daughters from the beginning, giving it whatever benefit I could of any knowledge of mine and of my experience in bookmaking, but my function has been merely editorial.

GATE OF PEKIN.

THE STORY OF COLUMBUS.

CHAPTER I.

MARCO POLO.
1254-1324.

In the middle ages people had never dreamed about such a place as America. To them the known world consisted of Europe, part of Asia, and a little strip of Africa. The first man to help people to know more about the world and to make them wish to know still more was a Venetian gentleman, named Marco Polo, who lived two hundred years before Columbus. Strangely enough, Marco Polo did something toward the discovery of America, though he journeyed by land rather than by sea, and traveled to the East instead of to the West.

When Marco Polo was born (about 1254) his father and uncle, Nicolo and Maffeo Polo, had just sailed away from Venice, which was their home, on a trading voyage to Constantinople. When they got to that city, instead of trading the goods which they had brought with them for some of the silks and spices which came from the far East and returning home as

GENERAL MAP OF MARCO POLO'S JOURNEY.

other merchants did, they exchanged all their merchandise for jewels, which could be concealed from robbers more easily than gold, and went on into the Eastern countries. I suppose they had some curiosity to find out where the spices, silks, gums, and jewels, which Europeans were so glad to buy, came from. They journeyed through Asia to China, or Cathay, as people called it in those days. The great Chinese Emperor, Kublai Khan, treated the strangers very kindly, and sent back a message by them to the Pope.

The travelers were gone nineteen years, and when they returned they found that Nicolo had a son named Marco whom they had never seen, although he had by this time grown to be a man. They stayed in Italy two years, and then they took Marco with them and set out for the empire of Kublai Khan once more, carrying some presents and letters from the Pope to the Chinese Emperor. It took the Polos four years to make the difficult and dangerous journey across Asia, to the home of the Grand Khan, who was very much delighted to see them. Marco became a great favorite with the Emperor, who made him one of his officers. While Marco Polo was traveling about China as an officer of Kublai Khan his father and uncle made themselves useful by building a catapult, which was a machine at that time in use in Europe for throwing stones and other missiles. Gunpowder had not yet been invented.

CATAPULT LOADED.

CATAPULT DISCHARGED.

When the Polos had been away from home about twenty years they grew homesick. They asked the Khan for permission to go back to Venice for a visit, but the Emperor was so fond of them that he at first refused. He finally consented to let them go, but he made them promise to return to China, giving them, at the same time, many rich presents and some tablets of gold, which they were to show as passports in the various countries that they would have to pass through. About this time the daughter of Kublai Khan was to be married to the King of Persia. The Khan sent the Polos as far as Persia in the fleet which carried this princess to her new home. The Chinese fleet touched at different points in the East Indies, and so the travelers had a chance to see something of the islands where spices grew. When they reached Persia they were entertained very magnificently for nine months. After this somewhat long wedding festival was over the Polos continued on their way to Europe, dressed in coarse Chinese costume, so that they might not be in danger of being murdered for their riches.

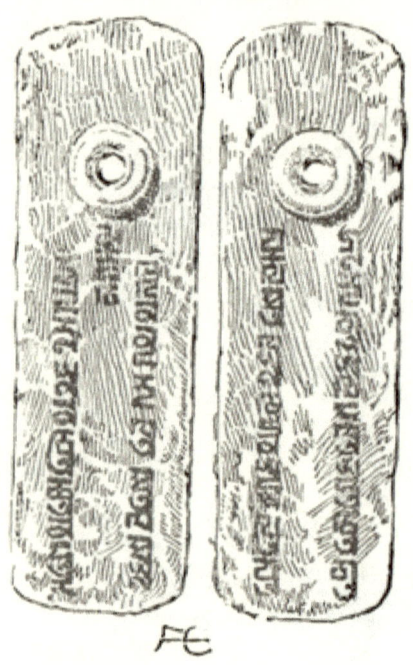

PASSPORT OF GOLD SUCH AS THE POLOS USED IN CHINA.

When they reached Venice, after having been gone twenty-four years, the travelers found that they had come to be regarded by their friends as long since dead and buried, and that their house had been inherited by

ARRIVAL OF THE POLOS IN VENICE.

some of their relatives. This was unpleasant for the three Polos, especially as the members of their family refused to believe that they were indeed themselves, which was not so strange, for the wanderers were very much tanned, wore coarse Chinese dresses, and spoke their own tongue like Chinamen.

The strangers, however, gave a dinner to which they invited all the gentlemen of the Polo family. When the guests arrived they found the travelers dressed in robes of crimson satin. No sooner had water been served for the washing of hands, after the fashion of those days, than the three strange Polos rose, left the room, and presently returned in robes of crimson damask. They caused the satin gowns to be cut up and divided among the servants. The guests probably thought this a very extravagant proceeding. However, the dinner had progressed but little further before the travelers again left the room and returned in crimson velvet robes, while the damask gowns were also distributed among the servants. After a time the three Polos left the room once more, and came back dressed as Venetians, causing the velvet suits to be cut up as the others had been. Finally, when the cloth was removed from the table and the servants dismissed, the travelers brought in the coarse Chinese dresses, which they had worn on their travels. Taking sharp knives, they cut open the seams of these old garments and took out rubies, carbuncles, emeralds, and diamonds. Before leaving China they had exchanged the wealth which Kublai Khan had given them for these jewels, so that they might carry their riches with them. The sight of so much wealth quite freshened the memories of the other members of the Polo family. They could no longer doubt that such rich men were their relations.

After this, many people came to visit Marco Polo, in order to talk with him about his travels. He used the word millions so much in describing the riches of Kublai Khan that they dubbed him Messere Marco Millione, or Mr. Marco Millions, as we should say, while his house is yet called "the court of the millions," for many people did not believe the strange tales of Mr. Marco Millions.

Marco Polo was afterward captured in a war between Venice and Genoa, and while he was in a Genoese prison he dictated an account of his travels to a fellow-prisoner, who wrote it down. This book became very famous. Many people doubted Marco Polo's stories about gold-roofed palaces and other fairy-like wonders, though we now know that his marvelous tales were many of them true. The reading of Marco Polo's travels set some thoughtful people to thinking about distant countries and to planning ways of reaching them, so that it was Marco Polo, instead of his father and uncle, who had to do with the making of great discoveries. The Polos were not the only Europeans who had wandered as far as China, but Marco Polo was the first to leave a careful account of what he saw and heard. After him there was an Englishman named Sir John Mandeville who made a similar journey, and also wrote about it. These two books were read much by studious men, who were curious to know more concerning the geography of the world.

CHAPTER II.

HENRY THE NAVIGATOR.
1394-1473.

A MAN who had much more to do with the discovery of America than did Marco Polo was Prince Henry of Portugal, though he too looked for an Eastern and not a Western world. This prince was born in 1394, nearly a hundred years before Columbus discovered America. He was the son of John I of Portugal. This king had seized the throne at a time when there was great dispute as to who had a right to it, and most of the people believed him to be the only man able and brave enough to save the country. He proved to be a great king. Queen Philippa, the mother of Prince Henry, was an English lady, a daughter of the famous John of Gaunt, and sister of the English King Henry IV. Prince Henry's parents were noble and high-minded people, and they gave their sons the best education to be had in that day.

PRINCE HENRY THE NAVIGATOR.

HENRY THE NAVIGATOR. 9

Henry was the third son of King John and Queen Philippa, and as it was not likely that he would ever become king, he had the more time to spend in such studies as he loved. When the three young men had come of age, King John and Queen Philippa wished them to be made knights. In order to become a knight a young man had first to do some brave deed with his sword, even though he were a prince. That his sons might have a chance to win knighthood, King John thought of giving tournaments for a whole year and inviting the knights of all nations to attend them. Tournaments, however, were but playing at war, and the king's Minister of Finance told him that, as this would be a very costly plan, it would be better to spend the money in attacking the Moorish city of Ceuta, which was opposite to the rock of Gibraltar, for it was thought in those days a Christian act to attack the infidel Moors.

POSITION OF CEUTA.

The young princes were better pleased to gain knighthood in true war; so everything was secretly made ready to attack Ceuta, and Queen Philippa had three jeweled swords made to present to her sons when they should be knighted. But before the fleet was ready to sail the queen fell ill and died, giving the swords to her sons on her deathbed. Instead of waiting to mourn long over her death, the king and princes set out on their expedition, for they knew that this valiant action would have pleased her best.

Twice the Portuguese fleet anchored before Ceuta, and twice it was scattered by storms. The Moors were much frightened when they first saw the Christian ships, but when they were a second time driven away by storms the people of Ceuta were thrown off their guard, for they thought that the vessels would never get together again. Prince Henry, after a great deal

ROCK OF GIBRALTAR.

of trouble, however, got the fleet assembled again, and the Portuguese ships anchored for the third time before Ceuta. When the Moors saw this they crowded the wall of the city on the side next the fleet with men, and lighted candles in all the windows, in order to discourage the Christians by making them think that there were a great many soldiers in the town. The Portuguese were indeed already discouraged by so bad a beginning, but the king and his sons held to their purpose.

The princes landed, each of them in command of a division of the army, fought their way in at three different gates, and took possession of several parts of the city. But their soldiers fell to plundering too soon, and the Moors, seeing the Christians off their guard, made a rush and tried to drive them from the town. Prince Henry held the narrow street where he was with but a handful of men, and once, left all alone, he fought the enemy single-handed. Presently a messenger went to the king and told him that his son Henry had fallen. The king only answered:

"Such is the end which soldiers must expect."

When evening came, however, and John I called a council, Prince Henry was there, and his father's face lighted up with joy when he saw him. The king offered to knight Henry first of the three princes, because he had proved himself so brave a soldier, but Henry begged that his older brothers should be honored before him.

All night long the soldiers made plunder of the gold, silver, spices, and fine stuffs to be found in the Moorish city, while one nobleman selected for his share more than six hundred columns of marble and alabaster and a dome, purposing to build with these a palace for himself in Portugal. When morning came, the streets ran with oil, honey, spices, butter, and preserves which had been wasted by the plunderers. The three princes were knighted in the great mosque on this day; the Moors, with their women and children, meanwhile climbed the mountains behind the city, bewailing their loss. While others were plundering, Prince Henry was learning from Moorish prisoners something about the interior of Africa and the coast of Guinea, which made him think of making some discoveries in these unknown parts.

After Henry returned home he was invited by kings of other countries to come and lead their armies, but instead of becoming a great warrior he liked better to give up his life to making discoveries. In his day peo-

A SHIP FROM AN OLD MANUSCRIPT.

ple imagined, when they thought anything about it at all, that Africa reached to the south pole, but Prince Henry began to have a notion that possibly Africa did not extend so far, and that ships might sail around it, and thus reach the rich world of the East. His second brother, Dom Pedro, or Prince Peter, as we should say, spent twelve years in traveling to what people then called the seven parts of the world—that is, to Palestine, Turkey, Italy, Hungary, Denmark, England, and other places in Europe. When he came home he brought with him the travels of Marco Polo and a map said to have been made by this famous traveler. So Henry read the book of Marco Polo, and it helped to make him wish to find the way to the East Indies and China.

Prince Henry went to live on a lonely promontory which ran out into the sea. There was nothing but sage brush growing on this barren place, because the waves in time of storm spouted up through holes in the rocky shore and fell in a salt spray over the land, so that no other plants could grow there. Here he studied, and sent out ship after ship, to find out all about the coast of Africa.

Before Henry's time vessels had sailed only in the Mediterranean and in the Atlantic Ocean along the coasts of Europe. Sailors were very timid and feared to leave the land far out of sight. The compass had only just come to be used. For a long time after it was discovered that a needle rubbed on a magnet would turn toward the polar star, sea captains were afraid to use this discovery in finding their way by sea, lest their sailors should suspect them of being magicians, for men imagined that so strange a thing must have been made by the help of evil spirits. Prince Henry interested himself in all things that could make it safer to sail in the great Atlantic, of which people knew so little and had so great a horror that they called it the "Sea of Darkness." He improved maps and spent great sums of money on voyages of discovery. Although he did not

sail on these voyages himself he came to be called
"Henry the Navigator."

Some of the nobles of Portugal, who troubled themselves but little about unknown parts of the world, complained about Prince Henry's useless expeditions to the coast of Africa, until the Madeira Islands were discovered by his ships, when they thought best to say no more.

In spite of all the efforts of Henry the Navigator, discovery went on slowly. He had to offer his captains great rewards to get them to round a new cape. The sailors of those days imagined strange monsters in unknown seas, and thought that at the equator nobody could live, and that there the water of the ocean boiled because of the great heat. Prince Henry had difficulty in getting his seamen to sail around Cape Bojador and thus to enter the tropics. They were for the most part content to go a little farther than the last ship had sailed, and return with some gold dust and negro slaves with which to make a profit on their voyages.

MAP OF THE PORTION OF THE AFRICAN COAST DISCOVERED BEFORE PRINCE HENRY'S DEATH.

Henry lived among seamen. He sent out gentlemen of his household, his cup bearer and his squires, as captains on his ships. Adventurous sailors from other countries came to him to be sent on voyages of discovery, while he entertained negro chiefs and dined

Gate of St. Andrea (Genoa) as it exists at present.

on ostrich eggs brought from Africa. When Prince Henry died, in 1473, the African coast had been explored to Cape Verd, but the way to India had not yet been found, though the Portuguese had begun to be hopeful of it, because the coast of Africa turned eastward from Cape Verd.

GATE OF ST. ANDREA, GENOA,
AS IT WAS IN THE TIME OF COLUMBUS.

CHAPTER III.

YOUNG COLUMBUS.
1446-1474.

A VENETIAN gentleman and a Portuguese prince had made great discoveries in unknown parts of the world, but the most wonderful of all discoveries was to be made by one who was neither prince nor gentleman, Christoforo Colombo, a Genoese weaver.

Christopher Columbus, as we call him, was born in the Italian city of Genoa, somewhere about 1446. His

GENOA AND ITS HARBOR.

father was called Domenico Colombo, and his mother's name was Susanna. His father was a weaver of wool, while his mother came also of a family of wool and silk weavers. After Columbus became famous, some writers tried to prove that he came of a noble family, but this is not true, for the Colombos, as they were called in Genoa, were simple working people. The father, three uncles, and several of the cousins of Christopher Columbus were weavers, while his only sister married a cheese merchant. The father of Columbus was always poor, often he had to go in debt for the wool which he worked up, and once he bought a little piece of land and agreed to pay for it in pieces of cloth, but he did not get it paid for. He worked at his trade until he was about seventy-five years old, and finally died in debt, though he lived long enough to know that his oldest son had made a great discovery.

A great deal of trouble has been taken to find the house which Domenico Columbus owned, where Columbus lived when he was a boy, and where he was probably born. It is a very narrow house, low and dark, and stands in a quarter of Genoa which was outside of the old city walls. In this quarter lived weavers of wool and silk, dressers of cloth, fullers, carders, dyers, and all people who made their living by working at the making of cloth. Thus we know what kind of neighbors the great dis-

HOUSE IN WHICH COLUMBUS LIVED AS IT IS AT PRESENT.

coverer had when he was a boy. The little house stood just without the gate of St. Andrea, and Columbus must have seen this fine old gate many times in a day.

On the lower floor of the narrow little house was the shop, which was open to the street, and here Domenico Columbus and his apprentices did their weaving, displaying their goods on a counter at the open front, and stopping work to sell to any customer who should chance to come. The family lived over the shop, and may have rented the story above this to some other poor family. The windows had no glass in them, but there were wooden shutters for cold weather, with small apertures in them, which let in light through oiled linen or paper.

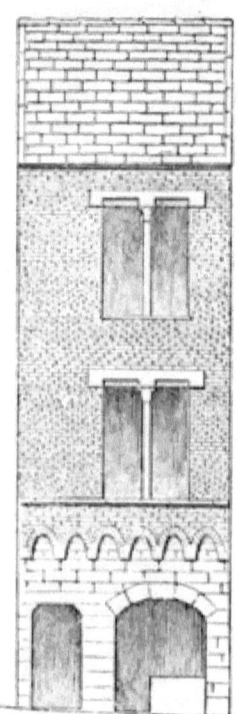

SUPPOSED APPEARANCE OF THE HOUSE IN COLUMBUS'S TIME. (STAGLIENO.)

The weavers of Genoa established little schools for their children, and probably Columbus was sent to one of these to learn to read, write, and cipher, until he got old enough to learn his father's trade. When this time came he went into his father's shop as an apprentice, and here he learned to comb wool or weave, probably both. Columbus had three brothers, who were apprenticed to learn the weaver's trade, like himself. In later life he shared his good fortunes with two of them, Bartholomew and Diego, while we know nothing of his other brother, except that he must have died when he was rather young.

In 1470, when Christopher Columbus was about twenty-four years old, he went on some small trading voyage, for he signed a contract to pay a man sixty dollars for some wine which Columbus was to take on board a vessel and trade at some other port in the Mediterranean. But he does not seem to have been yet much of a sailor, for he is still called a weaver in the old papers.

In Genoa a young man was not of age until he was twenty-five years old. About the time that Columbus came of age his father moved with his family to the city of Savona, and there set up a weaver's shop. Two years after the removal to Savona a young comrade of Christopher's, named Nicolo Monleone, who was also a weaver, died. Before Nicolo died, he made a will, to which there were six witnesses, three of whom were tailors, one a bootmaker, one a cloth-dresser, and one a weaver, this weaver being Christo-

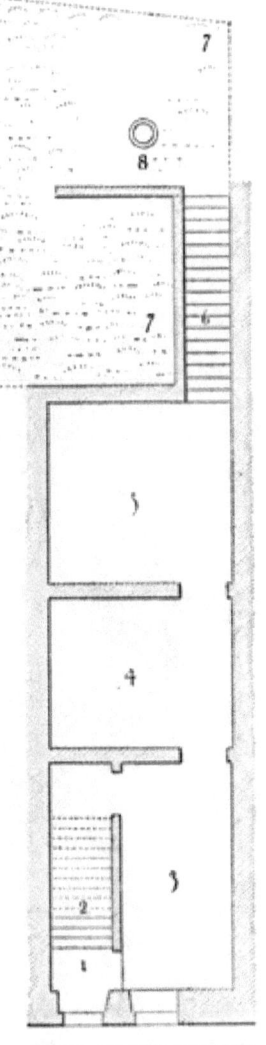

PLAN OF THE GROUND-FLOOR OF THE HOUSE IN WHICH COLUMBUS LIVED. (STAGLIENO.)

pher Columbus. From this we know that Columbus was yet a plain working man. Soon after this, the

CATHEDRAL OF SAN LORENZO, GENOA.

young weaver and his father signed a paper in which they agreed to pay for some wool in pieces of cloth.

Old legal papers, the only sources from which we can learn anything very certain about the early life of

Columbus, show that he lived in Savona as a weaver until 1473, when he must have been about twenty-seven years old. There can be no doubt, however, that Christopher Columbus was no common weaver's boy, for he had less than twenty years more in which to learn to be a great navigator as well as to become a man of considerable education. It is altogether likely that he had very

HARBOR OF SAVONA.

little schooling, and that, like other men who have been poor boys and become famous, he educated himself by hard study at odd times.

Genoa, like other Italian cities, had made itself rich by sending ships out to trade. All the land which belonged to this city was a very small province, hemmed in by mountains, and most Genoese men who wished to become rich or famous had to take to the sea. The province of Genoa had already furnished many admirals to Portugal, where such great discoveries were being pushed forward. No doubt Columbus, from the time that he was a little boy, had often stood on the wharves and seen the ships unloading their valuable merchandise, while he talked with seamen fresh from distant lands. He must have heard of Prince Henry's great plan for reaching India by going around Africa, and of the voyages made by the Portuguese. Perhaps he too had heard while he was still a weaver the story of Marco Polo's strange travels, for we know that at some time in his life he read Marco Polo's book, and that it made him wish very much to reach the rich countries about which it told.

It is certain that young Columbus had a lively imagination, as well as a great deal of ambition. No doubt he often fancied himself making such a strange journey as did Marco Polo, or sailing still farther than any Portuguese captain had done, and reaching the much-desired India. For him, as for many another Genoese young man, the sea was the only high road to fame and fortune, and Portugal was the place to go to if one wished to become a great discoverer, so when he was about twenty-seven or twenty-eight, Columbus gave up his trade forever and took to the sea. A few years later we find him in Portugal.

CHAPTER IV.

COLUMBUS IN PORTUGAL.
1474–1485.

There is very little known about the life of Columbus before he became a great man. We know that he went to live in Portugal, and that while he was there he made many voyages, for he afterward said that he had sailed in all the east, west, and north. It did not take a great deal of voyaging, however, to go into all the known seas of those days. Columbus had but to sail east in the Mediterranean, north to Iceland, south along the explored coast of Africa, and to the islands west of Africa and of Europe to be a very experienced sailor, for this was as far as Europeans had ventured in any direction. At some time in his early life he got a wound, perhaps in one of the sea fights common in that day. While Columbus was in Portugal he married a Portuguese lady, of good family, named Philippa Moniz.

Columbus was a tall, strong man, with a long face, brilliant blue eyes, an aquiline nose, red hair, and a ruddy complexion, marked with freckles. He was rather rough and abstracted in his manner, and somewhat quick-tempered, though he knew how to be amiable at times. Those who saw Columbus said that he was a fine-looking man, although he dressed almost as plainly as a monk, for he was too thoughtful to care much about his clothes.

24 THE STORY OF COLUMBUS.

He was very much interested in geography, and learned to make maps and globes, and he sometimes made his living by selling these. Perhaps while he was making spheres he thought a great deal about what was in the great blank spaces. He believed that the part of the world already known—that is, from the Canary Islands to a certain city in Asia—made two thirds of the distance

PORTRAIT OF COLUMBUS.

around the globe, and that, as Marco Polo said that Asia extended very far eastward, it must come quite a distance over into the unknown third of the world, and hence it would be quite easily reached by sailing west from Europe. In reality, only about one third of the world was known, while there remained two thirds to be explored; but learned men in those days made the same mistake concerning the size of the earth that Columbus did. Probably if the truth about the circumference of the world had been known, America would not have been found by Columbus.

We have seen that Columbus was born in an age of discovery. It was not so much a curiosity to know about the unknown parts of the earth that made men at first bent on discovery as it was the desire for wealth. Italian cities, like Genoa, where Columbus was born, and Venice, where Marco Polo lived, had become rich by sending out ships to trade with the Mohammedans, who sold spices, silks, and precious stones, which were brought by caravans from Asia. Those who had the means liked very much to dress in silk and jewels, while spices were greatly prized for seasoning the food of that day, which was rather plain and coarse. Great prices were paid for all kinds of goods from the East, and those who could sell them became rich, and enriched the countries where they lived. For this reason Prince Henry, as well as his brother and nephew, who were successively kings of Portugal, wished to find a way to India by sailing around Africa, thus making their country a market for the precious goods of the East. Spices and jewels, silks and precious gums, drew men around the world on long and dangerous voyages and led them to find out about the globe on which they lived.

It was probably while Columbus was in Portugal that he first thought of sailing directly west to reach Asia, instead of trying to go around Africa. He had not the least idea of finding a new continent, nor any desire to make such a discovery. Men in those days had no use for a new world; what they longed for was an old world where precious commodities not to be found in Europe could be procured.

In the days of Columbus many fables about islands in the Atlantic Ocean were believed. One of these stories was that when the Moors had conquered Spain, seven bishops with a great many people had sailed away into the Atlantic Ocean to an island where they had founded seven splendid cities, and the imaginary island on which they lived was called the Island of the Seven Cities. Another tale was about an island called St. Brandon, where a Scotch priest named St. Brandon had landed in the sixth century. People believed so firmly in these fantastic islands that the kings of Portugal several times gave them to subjects of theirs, who never could succeed in finding their possessions. An imaginary island in which the ancients had believed, called Antilla, was looked for. There was still another fabled island called Brazil, and an Englishman named Thomas Lloyd had sailed to the west of Ireland in 1480 in search of it. After about nine months Lloyd's ships put into an Irish port, badly beaten by tempests, and without having found the island of Brazil. People living on the Maderia Islands thought they saw on clear days a large island to the west, which they believed to be St. Brandon. They sent in search of it, having first taken care to procure a grant of St. Brandon, but their island was never found. In spite of such disappointments, St. Brandon, the Seven Cities, Antilla, Brazil, and other imaginary islands were put down on the maps of that day. Columbus made a careful note of all these tales. He too believed in the fabled islands, but he did not want to make a random voyage in search of them, as had other sailors. He only thought of them as convenient and encouraging stopping places in making the long voyage westward to the shores of Japan and China.

All that was known about Japan in the days of Columbus was that Marco Polo had reported that there was an island, which he called Cipango, lying five hundred leagues east of China. Marco Polo said that in Cipango there was an abundance of precious stones, while the king of that country lived in a palace the roof of which was covered with plates of gold, just as in Europe palaces are covered with plates of lead. This story is not impossible, since temples roofed with tiles of gold are not unknown in Asia to-day. Columbus did not doubt the stories of "Marco Millions," and he imagined himself sailing westward around the world, and so reaching the Island of Japan and the land of the Grand Khan. Thus the accounts of Marco Polo had much to do with both the discoveries of Prince Henry on the coast of Africa and with the finding of a new world in the West.

Columbus was not the only man who had the grand idea of sailing west to reach the East. A great astronomer named Paolo Toscanelli, who lived in Florence, had sent a letter to the Portuguese King, in which he said that India could be reached by a shorter way than that which the Portuguese were looking for around Africa, and that this voyage should be made by sailing always westward. Columbus wrote to Paolo Toscanelli on the subject, and the great astronomer sent him a copy of this letter. He also sent Columbus a map in which the shores of Asia were made to come opposite to the shores of Europe, while the imaginary Antilla and other islands, as well as the real Japan, dotted the ocean at convenient distances between the two continents. We see that though Columbus was not the only person who had the great idea, the difference between him and other men was that he believed so strongly in his idea that after he had once got it he thought of nothing else, and tried for nothing else but to carry it out.

Since he was to find rich heathen lands, which, according to the idea of those days, must be taken posses-

MAP OF THE SUPPOSED WESTERN HEMISPHERE.

sion of and converted to Christianity. Columbus thought it necessary to have a powerful king back of him. Besides this, he was far too poor a man to pay the cost of such an expedition alone. From the days of Prince Henry the Portuguese kings had known a great deal about navigation and had "great heart," as Columbus himself said, in undertaking voyages of discovery.

John II, the grand-nephew of Prince Henry, was now on the throne. The king entertained learned men, both Jews and Christians in his palace, and received mariners from all parts of the world. While he reigned some noble discoveries were made by his sailors.

Columbus had come to live in Portugal, the land of discovery. He carried his project to John II, proposing to him to find a way to the East Indies which should be shorter than the way he was seeking around Africa. The king kept Columbus waiting a long time, and at length declined his proposal. There were several reasons why so wise a king should have made this mistake. Columbus was a poor stranger, and Portugal did not need any longer to borrow its seafaring men from other countries, since there were now many hardy seamen in Portugal who had been taught in the school of African explorations. Then, too, Columbus, poor as he was, demanded great rewards for his discoveries; he would have nothing less than the vice-royalty of the lands which he should find, the title of admiral, and a tenth part of the profits. He meant to make himself rich as well as famous by his discoveries. King John did not give such high rewards, and he was also perhaps a little disappointed in the results of Portuguese explorations, which had cost more than they had brought in. As the Cape of Good Hope had not yet been found, the success of the attempt to reach India remained still in doubt. King John, however, did allow some of his own subjects to try a voyage westward, but they returned without having found land. This is said to have made Columbus very angry, for he felt that he had been cheated.

CHAPTER V.

COLUMBUS IN SPAIN.
1485–1487.

Columbus must have been very much disappointed when he was finally refused by King John, for Portugal was really the only country which was interested in discovery. But he was a persistent man, and he did not for a moment give up his plan. His brother Bartholomew had come to Portugal to try his fortunes with Christopher. Columbus now sent Bartholomew to propose the plan to the King of England and the King of France, while he himself set out for Spain. Knowing that Spain was jealous of the discoveries of the Portuguese, he hoped that the king and queen of this country would be pleased with the idea of outdoing her neighbor in the race for India. When Columbus left Portugal to seek his fortunes in Spain, somewhere about the year 1485, he left his wife and several little children behind him.

At the time when Columbus went to Spain it was

MAP OF PORTUGAL, SPAIN, AND GENOA.

governed by Ferdinand and Isabella. Before the time of this king and queen the country had been divided up into a great many kingdoms, and there were all sorts of disorders, while the Moors, who had once conquered all Spain, were at war almost continually with the Christians. But when Ferdinand, who was heir to the throne of Aragon, and Isabella, who became Queen of Castile, were married, and other small kingdoms came under their rule, Spain began to be, for the first time, a powerful country. Ferdinand and Isabella made it their chief work to conquer the Moors. At the time when Columbus came to Spain the Moors had been driven into the mountain kingdom of Granada, and here they were making their last stand against the Christians.

PORTRAIT OF KING FERDINAND.

PORTRAIT OF QUEEN ISABELLA.

King Ferdinand was a man of middle height, with muscles made hard and strong by exercises at arms. He had chestnut hair, a high forehead, which was also a little bald, crooked teeth, and a face burned by constant exposure in war. His voice was sharp, and his speech quick. He dressed very plainly, for both Ferdinand and Isabella disliked ostentation. When Ferdinand once wished to reprove a courtier for dressing too finely, he laid his hand on his own doublet and said:

"Excellent stuff this, it has lasted me three pairs of sleeves."

Ferdinand was an able king, careful and business-like. But Queen Isabella was much more loved than he. Her complexion was fair, her hair auburn, and her eyes blue and kindly. She was thought to be very beautiful. She was, when her religious bigotry was not aroused, a tender-hearted woman, and yet a queen of much ability and force. She governed her own kingdom, while Ferdinand governed his. During the wars with the Moors she sometimes busied herself with sending provisions to the army under command of the king, and sometimes rode into camp to encourage the soldiers. Several suits of steel armor which Isabella wore have been kept to this day. She rode great distances on horseback, and sometimes, after spending the day in business, she would sit up all night dictating dispatches.

This great king and queen were so busy with their war against the Moors that it was very hard for Columbus to get them to listen to his plans or to think about them long at a time. The Spanish court was a camp which moved from place to place as the war went on, and Columbus had to follow it about. When he proposed his project to King Ferdinand and Queen Isabella they called a council of the wisest men about the court to hear what the stranger had to say, and to decide whether it was possible to reach the islands of eastern Asia by sailing to the west. The court was then at the city of Salamanca, and it was during the winter of 1486-'87.

The council of wise men which listened to the reasons of Columbus for wishing to undertake so strange a voyage did not think it could be done. Ferdinand and Isabella did not, however, entirely refuse to consider the plans of Columbus, for he still followed the court when it moved to the city of Cordova. The account book of the royal treasurer of those days has been found,

SALAMANCA.

in which it is set down that on May 5, 1487, three thousand marevedis were paid to Cristobal Colomo, for this is what Columbus was then called in Spain. The three thousand marevedis would be about seventy-five dollars, but we must not forget that money would buy a great deal more in those days than now. In this old account book Columbus is set down as a stranger "employed in certain things for the service of their Highnesses." So we see that the poor foreigner who came to propose an unheard of project was treated with kindness.

It is not known how Columbus had earned his living in Spain before this, though it is told by some that he made maps, and by others that he sold printed books. Printed books were a new thing in those days, for printing had not been very long invented, and Queen Isabella was very much interested in promoting this new art.

CHAPTER VI.

COLUMBUS BEGS IN VAIN.
1487-1491.

For some years Columbus followed the Spanish court, trying to get the attention of the busy king and queen, who could not think long of anything but their war with the Moors. Sometimes he was noticed by great men at court. Quintanilla, the treasurer of the crown, pitied the poor foreigner, and gave him a home in his own house for a while. Diego de Deza, the bishop who taught the king's son, was kind to Columbus, and Juan Cabrero, who was first chamberlain to Ferdinand, befriended him. Sometimes the king and queen ordered money to be paid to him, or commanded the towns that he had to pass through in going to court to feed and lodge him. Still, there were times when Columbus was very poor and wore a shabby mantle. Many people laughed at his notions, and the very children are said to have pointed to their foreheads when he passed, to indicate that they thought him a crazy fellow.

While Columbus was following the bustling court from place to place, his wife and all of his children, except one little boy named Diego, died in Portugal. Columbus afterward had this little Diego with him in Spain. He had also another little son, whom he called

Ferdinand. The mother of this child was named Beatriz Enriquez, and lived in the city of Cordova.

Columbus was present when the king laid siege to the Moorish city of Malaga, which was a rich and beautiful town, adorned with lovely gardens. The people of Malaga held out very obstinately, and in order that they might know that the Christian army had come to stay,

CHILDREN MOCKING COLUMBUS.

Queen Isabella rode into the camp and took up her abode there. It is not very likely that any one thought much about the plans of Columbus during this busy time, but he was there waiting as usual. The people of

Malaga were finally starved out, the city surrendered, crosses and bells were put in the mosques, and the poor inhabitants were enslaved as a punishment for their stubborn courage.

Every year some great city was besieged and taken. The next year, which was 1489, it was the Moorish city of Beza. There were floods and a great scarcity of food this year, and it was so hard to get money that Queen Isabella is said to have pawned the crown jewels and even the crown itself in order to carry on the war. The lack of money, the continuance of the war, and the great preparations for the wedding of the Princess Isabella, the daughter of Ferdinand and Isabella, made it useless for Columbus to try to gain the attention of the sovereigns. Disheartened, he turned away from the Spanish court, intending to go to France or England to look for help. There was, however, in Spain, a nobleman called the Duke of Medina-Celi, who was himself almost a king, for he owned vessels and seaports, as well as great lands. This duke befriended Columbus in his time of discouragement. He took the poor foreigner into his own house to live, and kept him for two years among the many retainers that a great lord was accustomed to keep about him in those days. The duke was interested in the project of Columbus, and thought to let the stranger have three or four vessels at his own cost, since that was all he needed to try his novel voyage. The ships were made ready, but the duke dared not go into this undertaking without first letting the monarchs know about it. He wrote to the queen to ask her permission, but she declined to allow the duke to send out the ships on his own account.

Columbus returned to court. Perhaps he hoped that if the queen cared enough for his project to refuse to let a subject undertake it she would carry it out herself. She did appoint the treasurer, Quintanilla, to examine the proposal of Columbus. But the king and queen were making great preparations to lay siege to the city of Granada, and Columbus was once more forgotten. He followed the Spanish court to the encamp-

VIEW OF THE ALHAMBRA ACROSS GRANADA.

ment before Granada. Queen Isabella, dressed in armor, rode about the field on a beautiful horse, reviewing her troops. Once the fine tent in which she slept caught fire, and the queen and her children were barely saved from burning. Because of this accident, and for the reason that winter was coming on, the queen resolved to build solid houses of stone and mortar for the encampment, so that there should be a city outside of a city. In less than three months, the new city had sprung up, which was called Santa Fé, or Holy Faith. Amid all this tumult of work there was no hope for the poor Genoese. Columbus was out of money and discouraged. His brother Bartholomew had been to England, where Henry VII was king, and had got some encouragement there. He had then gone to France, where he was kindly received by Anne de Beaujeu, who governed for her young son, Charles VIII. So Columbus resolved to journey either to France or England, perhaps to both of these countries, and see what he could do.

CHAPTER VII.

A FRIENDLY MONK.
1491.

It was quite likely that Columbus would have to wait many years before he could prevail on the rulers of England or France to undertake his discovery. It was therefore necessary that he should provide for his children as well as a poor man could. Ferdinand Columbus was very young yet, and might be left with his mother, but Columbus must find a home for Diego. He made up his mind to take him to the town of Huelva, where the child had an uncle and aunt, who could take care of him.

Columbus and his little boy traveled on foot. He had almost reached the town of Huelva when he stopped one day at the monastery of La Rabida, and begged the porter to give him a little bread and water for the child. The prior of the convent, named Juan Perez, happened to see Columbus, and noticed that the poor stranger spoke Spanish with the accent of a foreigner.

"Who are you, and where do you come from?" asked the prior.

"I have come," answered Columbus, "from the court, where I have been to propose certain maritime discoveries, engaging myself to make land at *terra firma*, and demanding that they confide an expedition to me for this purpose. But the men of the court have turned my projects into derision, saying they were nothing but air bubbles. Despairing of success, I have left the court, and am going to Huelva, to the house of a man named Muliar, husband of a sister of my wife."

The good monk wanted to hear what the plan of Columbus was. So he invited him into the monastery,

WITH JUAN PEREZ AT THE MONASTERY.

and made him tell his story. Then he sent for a certain doctor of medicine, named Garcia Hernandez, who lived near by, in the town of Palos. This doctor knew something of the science of astronomy, and astronomy had much to do with geography in those days, for it was still rather a strange thing to believe that the world was round, and it took something of an astronomer to have faith in such an opinion.

The shabby stranger, the monk, and the doctor had a long talk together, which ended in the monk's believing in the possibility of the bold project of Columbus. This same Juan Perez had once been confessor to Queen Isabella. So he wrote a letter to the queen, begging her not to let Columbus leave Spain from discouragement. A pilot, named Sebastian Rodriguez, carried the letter to court, while Columbus and the little Diego stayed in the friendly convent. After fourteen days, Rodriguez came back with an answer from the queen, asking Juan Perez to come to court and talk with her. So the good Perez saddled his mule and set off secretly in the night to the court, which was still in the city of Santa Fé, before Granada.

We do not know why Juan Perez made his journey so privately, nor what he said to the queen when he saw her once more, but we know that his friendship was worth more to Columbus than the friendship of all the great courtiers who had been kind to him at different times. The queen sent Perez back for Columbus, and at the same time she sent the navigator about seventy-two dollars, which would be the same in value as two hundred and sixteen dollars in our day. With part of this money Columbus made haste to buy some decent clothes and a mule, while he kept the rest to pay his traveling expenses. He and Juan Perez journeyed back to Santa Fé together with light hearts.

After they reached court, Queen Isabella appointed a conference of learned men to decide once more about the scheme of Columbus. There was a great discussion among these men. As for sailing partly around the

A WINDOW IN THE ALHAMBRA.

world, some did not think it could be done and others were in favor of trying it. The Church fathers were quoted to prove that there could be no human beings living on the opposite side of the earth. According to their notions, the people of Europe lived on the top of the ball and it was impossible for men to exist on the other side of the world, since they would have to walk

GATEWAY OF GRANADA.

upside down. How was it possible for trees to grow with their roots above them, and how could it rain and snow upward? So strong was the notion that they lived on the top of the earth that, years after, Columbus was said to have discovered "a considerable portion of the lower world."

In the midst of this assembly sat Cardinal Mendoza, who was called the Third King of Spain, because he was so powerful. Just behind him sat Geraldini, the bishop who taught the royal children. Geraldini remarked to the great cardinal that the Church fathers were no doubt excellent theologians, but only mediocre geographers, since the Portuguese had reached a point in the other hemisphere where they could no longer see the polar star, and had discovered another star at the south pole, and yet they had found all the countries situated under the torrid zone perfectly peopled.

The great cardinal favored the project of Columbus, and so did most of the assembly. About this time the city of Granada surrendered, and the war with the Moors was at an end. The flag of Spain floated from the highest tower of the beautiful palace called the Alhambra. Columbus saw Boabdil, the last of the Moorish kings, come forth and kiss the hands of Ferdinand and Isabella, and of the young prince Juan, who was heir to the throne. Ferdinand and Isabella had made themselves the greatest sovereigns in Christendom, but they never once imagined that the discoveries of this poor Genoese weaver, who had so long followed their court and waited disconsolately in their ante-rooms, would add more to the glory of their reign than their great Moorish conquest.

CHAPTER VIII.

GETTING READY FOR THE VOYAGE.
1492.

It was in the very beginning of the year 1492, after he had waited seven years in Spain, that Queen Isabella agreed to send Columbus to seek a new way to India. But there was still another disappointment in store for the ambitious adventurer. He asked great rewards—the titles of admiral and viceroy and a share in the profits arising from all the discoveries he should make. This was too much, and Columbus would take nothing less, so he turned his back once more on the Spanish court, resolved to go immediately to France. After he had gone, Luis de Santangel, an officer of King Ferdinand's Kingdom of Arragon, is said to have remonstrated with Queen Isabella for letting such an opportunity slip. The queen relented, and a courier was sent to bring back the disappointed Columbus as he rode slowly away on his mule So the poor man with the grand projects returned to court once more, and this time no objections were made to his demands.

There was some trouble about raising money enough to send Columbus on his voyage. The queen wished him to wait until the Moors were expelled from Spain, when the treasury would be filled with the money taken from the conquered people. But Columbus would

GETTING READY FOR THE VOYAGE. 47

wait no longer. There is a story that Queen Isabella offered to raise the money that was needed by pawning her jewels, but this is not probable, since the queen's jewels had been already pawned, it is thought, to carry on the war. At this moment, when the plans of Columbus were likely to fail for want of a little money, Luis de Santangel offered to lend the money to the queen.

It would seem that King Ferdinand did not believe in the project of Columbus, for he did not share in the undertaking, and for some time after the discovery of America only the Castilians, who were Isabella's own subjects, were allowed to send ships there.

At last the papers were signed. Columbus was to have the title of admiral and the office of viceroy over the lands that he should discover. He was to have a tenth part of the gold, precious stones, pearls, silver, spices, and other articles found in these lands, and if he bore an eighth part of the expenses he was to have an eighth part of the profits of all the voyages made, while he and his family were to have the title of Don, which was a great honor in those days, something like the title of Lord in English.

After all the long delays and the many doubts as to whether it was best to undertake this famous first voyage of Columbus, it cost Queen Isabella only about sixty thousand dollars. Columbus furnished one of the three small ships which were to sail, and so did his share toward the expenses. We do not know who it was that lent to Columbus the money to do this, for he was certainly too poor to do it himself.

The little town of Palos, which was near the monastery of La Rabida, had done something for which it was punished by being obliged to furnish two ships every year to the crown. So the order was now given that Palos should turn over its two ships to Columbus. The royal order was read in the church of St. George in Palos to the officers of the town and many of the people. They promised to furnish the ships without any trouble, but when it was found that they were to sail into unknown seas there was great horror. The owners of the vessels thought that they would certainly lose their ships, while common sailors refused to go on any such voyage. When courtiers and learned men were so uncertain about the undertaking, it is not strange that it was altogether terrible to ignorant people. Some of the men at court are said to have thought that when Columbus had once sailed west, he would find the roundness of the earth like a mountain, which he could not sail up again to come home. The sailors of Palos probably knew nothing about the earth being round, but they had many strange beliefs about the Sea of Darkness, as the Atlantic was called, and they thought that they would never see Spain again if they ventured off in this waste of waters.

When Queen Isabella heard of this new difficulty, she sent a royal officer to see that ships were pressed into the service, and offered to let criminals out of the prisons if they would sail on the dreaded voyage. But still there was a great deal of trouble to get ships and men. A family of bold seamen, called Pinzon, took an interest in the expedition, however, and went to a great deal of trouble to find men to go as sailors.

At last ships were found. Two of them were of

the kind of vessel called caravels, and were not any larger than the small craft which one sees to-day sailing in rivers or coasting. Only the largest of them was decked over, the others were merely open sailing boats, with cabins built on the bow and stern, one being a very small craft with lateen sails. There was a great deal of trouble before the ships could be got ready. The men who calked them did

A CARAVEL.

it badly and then ran away; some of the sailors deserted and concealed themselves; the owners of the vessels were also willing to put obstacles in the way of the voyage.

But everything was ready by the beginning of August, 1492. Columbus was to sail in the largest ship, which was called the Santa Maria, that is Holy Mary, or as it was sometimes called The Marigalante, which means The Gallant Mary. This ship belonged to a man named Juan de la Cosa, who went along in command of her. The second ship, which was the best sailer, was called the Pinta. Her captain was Martin Alonzo Pinzon, one of the family who had helped Columbus to fit out for the voyage, while another Pinzon was pilot. This ship belonged to two men of Palos, named Gomes Rascon and Cristobal Quintero. These two owners also sailed in their ship, as though they could not bear to part company with their property on so dangerous an expedition, and, in fact, they meant to take the first opportunity to fetch the vessel back to

Spain. The smallest ship, called the Nina, was commanded by another of the bold Pinzon family. The sailors were a very mixed lot. Some of them were released prisoners, who would rather risk the horrors of unknown seas than take their punishment at home; and we find that there was even one Englishman and one Irishman in the motley company.

Before Columbus sailed he placed his two little boys, Diego and Ferdinand, at school in the city of Cordova. Diego was appointed a page to Prince Juan, the son of the king and queen. This was an honor which was usually granted only to the children of noble houses. The little Diego, who was probably about ten years old at this time, had to be sent to school for two years before he was fit to go to court and serve as page to a prince.

Every one who was to sail on the expedition took the sacrament before going. There were about ninety people in all. Letters were sent from the King and Queen of Spain, addressed to the Grand Khan, or Emperor of China, whom Columbus expected, without doubt, to find. An interpreter was provided who was supposed to speak Latin, Greek, Hebrew, Arabic, Coptic, and Armenian, for no one thought of anything but of the possibility of reaching Eastern lands. There was a sad parting at Palos, for the friends of those who sailed had little hope of ever seeing them again. The three little ships got under way at half an hour before sunrise on the morning of the 3d of August, 1492.

CHAPTER IX.

THE FIRST VOYAGE OF COLUMBUS.
1492.

No doubt it was a moment of relief to Columbus when he found himself fairly at sea, where his men could not desert nor ship owners make any more delays; but the ship owners were with him, and his joy was short-lived. Rascon and Quintero, the proprietors of the Pinta, contrived, it is said, to have her rudder broken and unhung. The Pinta made signals of distress and the fleet was detained in a high sea. Martin Alonzo Pinzon, who was captain of the Pinta, tied the rudder with ropes, but it gave way again next day. There was nothing to do but to stop at the Canary Islands. Columbus tried to get another ship here, but as he could not do this he had the Pinta repaired, and at the same time had the lateen sails of the Nina changed so that she could keep up with the other ships.

Columbus spent about three weeks at the Canary Islands. While there he heard that some Portuguese ships were seen hovering off Ferro Island. Afraid that the Portuguese had heard of his expedition and that they might try to intercept him, Columbus got away as quickly as possible. For two days he lay becalmed, however, between the islands of Gomara and Tenerife. The sailors watched the volcano of Tenerife smoking day and night. They had never seen anything of the sort before, and the sight is said to have awakened many fears, but Columbus explained it to them and told them about Mount Etna.

On the 8th of September, at three o'clock in the morning, the wind sprang up and the three little ships were at length off for the New World. When they saw the last of the Canaries the sailors sighed and sobbed, for they thought they were doomed men; but

PEAK OF TENERIFE.

Columbus talked to them about the great countries to which they were sailing, and inflamed their minds by the promise of riches for them all. He saw that he was in danger of failing because his men were faint-hearted, so he did everything that he could to encourage them. He kept two reckonings of the distance the ships had sailed—one for the sailors, which he made every day some leagues shorter than the actual distance, and a secret reckoning for himself, which gave the true distance made. He did this because he knew that the men would be disheartened if they knew how far they were from home.

Three days after the ships left the Canary Islands a piece of a mast was picked up. It had lain long in the water, and seemed to have belonged to some large ship. Perhaps some vessel had tried these seas before and been lost. The men did not like the looks of this. Three days later Columbus noticed that the needle of the compass did not point directly toward the north star. He had never heard of the variation of the needle, now so well known to all mariners, and he was at a loss to understand it as many learned men have been since. In a few days the pilots noticed it and were anxious, for if the compass should fail them in this unknown ocean what would they do? But Columbus had invented a theory to explain it, and made use of it to reassure the pilots.

The fleet presently entered the region of the trade winds which blow steadily from east to west, following the course of the sun. The ships were blown gently westward, while the air was so sweet and mild that Columbus said it would have been like April in Andalusia or southern Spain if one might but have heard the song of the nightingale. A heron and a water-wagtail flew over the vessels and rejoiced the hearts of the men, for they thought that these birds would not fly far away from land.

The ships at length began to sail past great patches of green and yellow weeds floating on the water. Surely these weeds must have come from some island or reef. On one of the patches Columbus found a live crab. He kept it very carefully, for it was encouraging to see life in this great waste of waters. When night came on the ships plowed through schools of tunny fish, and the sailors amused themselves by throwing the harpoon at them. The crew of the Nina succeeded in killing one of these fish with a harpoon.

The smallest things were noticed on this first adventurous voyage. At three hundred and sixty leagues

THE CANARY ISLANDS AND THE AZORES.

from the Canaries another water-wagtail was seen. The weather continued to be mild. There was a gentle breeze, while Columbus said that the sea was as calm as the river Guadalquiver at Seville. The Pinta, being the best sailer, pushed ahead. Presently she waited for the admiral's ship, and Pinzon, who was her captain, called out that he had seen a great many birds flying toward the sunset and also that he had seen land covered with clouds to the north; but Columbus would not turn out of his course to look for land, though his men wanted him to. He believed in land to the west, and he did not wish to waste his time in sailing hither and thither. The wind began to freshen and the sailors had to shorten sail for the first time in a dozen days.

The next day there were drizzling showers, which Columbus thought were a sign that land was near. Two pelicans lit on the ships, and he told his men that these birds did not often fly twenty leagues from shore. Perhaps the ships were passing between islands, but still Columbus would not change his course. He sounded, however, with a line two hundred fathoms long, but there was no bottom, and this certainly did not look as though land were near.

The men had for a long time been discontented in spite of drizzling showers, weeds, live crabs, and water-wagtails. They were long out of sight of land, no other ships had ever sailed in these seas, so that there was no hope of rescue if they got into trouble. They did not like it that the wind blew always from the stern of the ship, for if the wind blew always one way how were they to reach home when they turned about? Then, too, they were afraid that the ships might be caught in one of those great fields of tangled weeds as they had heard of ships being caught in frozen seas.

It is not strange that the sailors were frightened. Many of them had been forced into this most audacious sea adventure that the world had ever known. Each day that they were disappointed in looking for land they thought how much farther they were from home. They had already sailed quite far enough to have made theirs one of the most wonderful of voyages.

One day there was a light wind blowing from the southwest, which was lucky for Columbus, for it proved that the wind did not always come from the east. Three little birds, which the men thought must have come from groves or orchards, lit singing on the masts in the morning and flew away again at night. Big birds, it was thought, might fly very far out to sea, but it was impossible that these tiny creatures would venture very far. Still, no land was seen and the breezes from the southwest were so light that they scarcely ruffled the water. The men began to complain that they could never reach home with such feeble winds. Columbus tried to encourage them; but when he had begun to be afraid that he could not restrain them much longer, there came up a great wind from the northwest, and the sea was quite rough enough to satisfy any one that the wind did not always blow from one quarter.

This same day a dove flew over the ships, and toward evening the men saw a pelican, a little river bird, and a white bird. There were also several live crabs on the floating weeds, and they discovered fishes swimming about the ships. Columbus made the most of every sign that land was near, but, under such circumstances, men grew tired of signs. The sailors began to say to one another that the admiral was a foreigner, who, for the mere fancy of making himself a great name and being called Don, made a game of exposing them to the greatest dangers and leading them to certain death. If Columbus would not consent to return, they might throw him in the sea, and say that he had fallen in while gazing at the stars, as was his habit.

Meantime the wind was favorable again on the 25th of September and the air was soft and mild. The vessels sailed near each other, while Columbus talked with Pinzon, the captain of the Pinta, about the map which Columbus had brought with him and which Pinzon had borrowed a day or two before. Pinzon thought that they might now be near Japan. Columbus agreed with him, but thought that the currents of the ocean might have carried the ships out of their course. He wished to look at the map again. Pinzon tied a rope to it and threw it on board the admiral's ship. While Columbus and his pilot were studying the map, Pinzon, who was standing on the high stern of the Pinta, shouted:

"Land! land! Señor, I claim my reward!"

The reason that Pinzon said this was that the king and queen had offered a velvet coat and a pension to the one who should first see land; but he who gave a false alarm could not claim the reward again. The captain of the Pinta pointed to the southwest. Yes, every one saw land there. Columbus threw himself on his knees and thanked God. It was growing dark, so he ordered that the ships should head toward the land in the night; but in the morning there was no land to be seen. Pinzon had been deceived again by sunset clouds.

The ships sailed on with a soft wind and a calm sea. In spite of their disappointment the sailors amused themselves by swimming about the ships. The men began to see dolphins, while flying fish fell on the decks of the ships. Four water-wagtails lit on the admiral's ship. So many birds of a kind, said Columbus, would not have ventured far from land. The Nina was the next to discover land, but it was again a false alarm. There began to be great flocks of birds flying over the ships. The sailors, however, were disheartened and would hear no more of signs. They had been a month out of sight of land, always on the lookout, and yet the sun rose day after day out of the boundless water and set again in the ocean. At sunset Columbus noticed that the birds all flew toward the southwest as though they were going to their roosting place, which must be on land. Remembering that the Portuguese had often found land by following the flight of the birds at sunset, Columbus changed his course to the southwest.

The 11th of October came. The air was sweet with land odors, fresh weeds floated by the ships, while the men saw a kind of green fish which lives about rocks. But, better than all, they picked up a thorny branch with red berries growing on it which was freshly broken from the tree. Then, too, they found a reed, a small board, and a stick which had been carved by hand. Even the discontented men could not doubt that land was near. In the evening, after all hands had sung the *Salve Regina* as usual, Columbus made his men a little speech, in which he told them how good God had been to bring them so far safely, telling them that as they had that day seen such sure signs of land they had better keep a lookout during the night.

CHAPTER X.

LAND AT LAST.

1492.

No eyes were closed on board the three little ships that night. The Pinta pushed ahead as usual. All were eagerly on the lookout. About ten o'clock, Columbus, who was standing on the high poop of his ship, saw a faint, trembling light. It appeared and disappeared, as though it might be a torch in a fisherman's boat which was being tossed up and down on the water, or perhaps a small candle being carried from one house to another on land. At two o'clock in the morning a gun was fired by the Pinta. A sailor on board this ship had seen land. The sails were now furled and the men spent the hours till daylight in rejoicings. Columbus must have been the happiest of them all. The poor weaver had made himself one of the greatest of men by the success of this voyage.

It was the 12th of October, 1492. After having been thirty-three days out of sight of land, Columbus and his men saw at daylight a low island covered with beautiful tropical trees, blooming and bearing fruit at a time of the year when the leaves were falling in Spain. It is not known to-day which island in the West Indies is the one at which Columbus first landed. It is a question between Watling's Island, Grand Turk

Island, Cat Island, Mayaquana, Samana, and Acklin's Island.

It was soon evident that the island was peopled, for men were seen running out of the woods to look at the ships. The Spaniards were, no doubt, too much delighted to see green land once more to be disappointed

MAP SHOWING THE ISLANDS AT WHICH COLUMBUS LANDED.

when they found that these men were naked, and that nothing was to be seen of the magnificent cities of Japan.

The ships' boats were manned, and the Spaniards made haste to the shore, carrying the flags of the expedition, which had a green cross on one side and the initials of Ferdinand and Isabella, surmounted by crowns, on the other side. Columbus had dressed himself richly in scarlet for this great occasion. When the boats touched shore, admiral and men leaped out, threw themselves on the earth, and kissed it. Columbus, when he had arisen, solemnly took possession of the island in the name of the king and queen and called it San Salvador, or Holy Saviour. He was then greeted by his men as

OLD PRINT OF 1500, SHOWING COLUMBUS LANDING AND THE KING OF SPAIN SENDING SHIPS ACROSS TO AMERICA.

viceroy of this new world, and they humbly begged his pardon for any offenses they had given him during the voyage.

The naked Indians assisted at the ceremony by staring very hard, having not the smallest idea that their country was being taken possession of. It is said that when the natives first saw the ships in the early morning, they thought them some kind of strange animal. Now, however, they imagined that these men had come down from the sky by means of the wings which they saw on their ships. After they had got a little used to the strangers they came near them, touching their beards, and wondering at the whiteness of their hands and faces. Columbus was pleased with the gentle, simple ways of these islanders. He gave them red caps, necklaces of glass beads, and other such things as the Portuguese used in trading with the negroes of Guinea. The Indians were delighted with their gifts, and made haste to put the strings of beads around their necks to enjoy the effect.

After resting on shore all day, Columbus and his men returned to their ships. Meantime the news was spreading among the natives, and each one was anxious to get some treasure of the men from the skies before they flew away again in their winged boats. They paddled up to the fleet in canoes or swam out, bringing live parrots and great balls of cotton yarn to exchange for anything the white men would give them. They were ready to give the few gold ornaments they had for a piece of broken dish, a scrap of glass, an end of a strap, or a bit of a barrel hoop; but Columbus would not let his men trade with the Indians for anything less valuable than beads or bells. When night came the Indians disappeared, only to swarm about the ships again when day returned. Their canoes were made of the trunks of trees hollowed out. They turned over very easily, but this did not trouble the natives, for they had no clothes to wet, and they swam about in the warm water until they could right their boats once more, baling the water out with calabashes. After a day or two the Indians began to feel themselves at home on the ships, and those who had nothing to trade would seize some trifle which had taken their fancy and, jumping overboard, swim ashore with it.

Columbus explored the coast of the island for some distance in the ships' boats. As the white men coasted the island, natives came out from the woods to see them, and ran along shore after them, offering them food and trying to get them to come to land. As they did not do this, the Indians swarmed about them in canoes or swam to them, making signs to them to know whether they had come down from the sky. Columbus was pleased with their simplicity, and gave them pins and other trinkets, with which they were highly delighted. After exploring part of the shore of the island, he resolved to push on for China or Japan.

Marco Polo had said that there were over seven thousand islands extending along the coast of Asia, where spices and scented woods grew. Columbus thought that he must be among these islands, and it only remained to find Japan, or the country of the Grand Khan—that is, China. Columbus asked the Indians where they got their gold ornaments, and, as they pointed toward the southwest and seemed to say something about a great monarch who used dishes of gold, he decided to go in search of this desirable king. Columbus carried away seven of the natives of San Salvador to teach them Spanish and make use of them as interpreters. He noticed that these men were not nearly so dark as the negroes of Africa, while their hair was not curly, but flowing. Some of them were covered with red, white, and black paint, others were only colored about the eyes and nose.

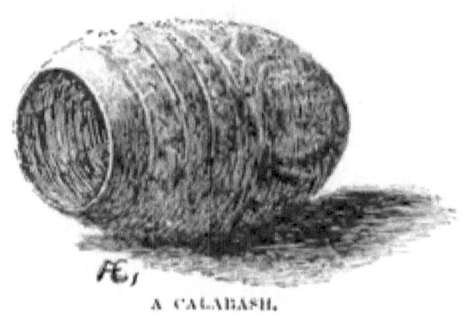

A CALABASH.

CHAPTER XI.

EXPLORING IN THE WEST INDIES.

1492.

Columbus could see many islands from his ship, and it was hard to decide which one to visit first. His Indian guides seemed to say by signs that at a neighboring island the natives wore bracelets and anklets of gold, so Columbus sailed for this. He landed and took possession with the same ceremonies that he had used on San Salvador, calling the island Santa Maria. Santa Maria proved to be very much like the first one; the natives were quite as much astonished, they were quite as naked, and gold was quite as scarce. So Columbus decided to proceed to another and much larger island. As the ships were about to sail, one of his Indian guides, who was on board the Nina, seeing that the white men were going so far away from his home on San Salvador, jumped into the water and swam to a canoe full of natives which was near. The sailors gave chase, but the Indians were too quick for them. They paddled ashore and ran into the woods, while the men took their revenge by capturing their canoe and tieing it behind the Nina. Columbus regretted this incident, since he did not want the Indians to be afraid of the white men. A canoe was approaching the ships from another part of the island with one native in it. This fellow was coming to trade a ball of cotton yarn for some hawk's shells. He stopped when he got near the ships, and seemed afraid to come nearer. Two or three sailors jumped overboard and captured him. Columbus stood on the poop of his ship. He ordered the Indian to be brought to him. The poor fellow came trembling and holding out his ball of yarn as an offering. But Columbus put a red cap on his head, strings of green beads about his arms, and hung little bells on his ears. He then had the fellow put in his canoe with his ball of cotton yarn and set free. He also made the sailors of the Nina let the canoe go that they had captured, so that the Indians to whom it belonged might find it again.

The ships now made for the larger island, and presently they ran across an Indian alone in a canoe, paddling across the wide gulf between the islands. He had a little cassava bread, which was the chief food of these

INDIAN PADDLING IN A DUG-OUT.

people, and a gourd of water for supplies. He had also a little red earth with which to paint himself on his arrival, and some dry leaves, which the white men thought were medicine. It is quite likely that they were leaves of tobacco. He wore a string of the white men's beads around his neck, and was no doubt paddling to other islands to astonish the natives with his finery, and to tell the story of how he had got it. As he seemed tired with paddling so far, the Spaniards took him on board, canoe and all. They fed him on bread, honey, and wine. The sea was so calm that the fleet did not reach the large island until night. The ships lay to until morning, but they put out the Indian boatman with his canoe, his treasures, and some presents, which Columbus had given him. He paddled ashore, and soon spread the news of the kindness of these strangers. The natives began coming out to the ships in the night, bringing fruit, roots, and spring water. Columbus gave them trinkets, and when any of them came on board, he gave him sugar and honey to eat, sweets being a great novelty to the Indians.

Columbus named the island Fernandina, for the king. The people of this island sometimes wore a cotton mantle over the shoulders, or a sort of apron tied around the waist. Their houses were circular bowers, made of branches, reeds, and palm leaves. Under these tent-like roofs were nets made of cotton cord, stretched from one post to another, for beds. The Indians called these beds *hamacs*, and so it is from these simple people that we get our hammock, even to the name.

The admiral sailed along the shore of Fernandina. While the men landed to fill their water barrels, Columbus went ashore and walked about. The great tropical forests filled him with admiration. "The country," said he, "was as fresh as the month of May in Andalusia; the trees, the fruits, the herbs, the flowers, the very stones, for the most part, as different from those of Spain as night is from day." The Indians made haste to fill the casks for their visitors from cool springs or little brooks.

Columbus sailed away from Fernandina in search of an island which the Indians described by signs as having a gold mine, and also a king who dressed in fine stuffs and wore golden ornaments. He discovered an island which he called Isabella. "There came off a fragrance," said Columbus, "so good and soft of the flowers and trees of the land that it was the sweetest thing in the world." He landed on this island without finding any sign of either gold mine or king, but he was delighted with the country. "I know not where first to go," he said, "nor are my eyes ever weary of gazing on the beautiful verdure. The singing of the birds is such that it seems as if one would never desire to depart hence. There are flocks of parrots which darken the sun, and other birds, large and small, of so many kinds and so different from ours that it is wonderful; and, besides, there are trees of a thousand species, each having its particular fruit and all of a marvelous flavor, so that I am in the greatest trouble in the world because I do not know them, for I am very certain that they are each of great value." Columbus did not doubt that many of these strange growths which he saw would be much prized in Spain for medicines and spices. He thought that he was in the East Indies, where valuable herbs and well-known spices grow. He did not fancy for a moment that he was in a new world where the plants were strange to Europeans, who had yet to learn their use and value.

When the admiral asked the Indians of this island where gold was to be found, they pointed south and said something about a large island called Cuba. He understood by their signs that there were gold, pearls, and spices there, and that large ships came there to trade. These, he made no doubt, were the ships of the Grand Khan, and the island must be Cipango or Japan. Columbus thought to sail there and load up with gold and precious stones. He purposed then to sail to China, where he would deliver his letters to the Grand Khan, and return in triumph into Spain.

CHAPTER XII.

COLUMBUS VISITS CUBA.

1492.

When Columbus neared the northern coast of Cuba he found that it was very large, with high mountains, beautiful valleys, and fine rivers. He landed in the mouth of one of these rivers and named the island Juana, after the little Spanish prince Juan, in whose suite his son Diego was to be a page. Two cabins stood near the place at which the Spaniards landed. The people who lived in them fled into the forest when they saw the strange visitors approaching. On examining the cabins the seamen found nothing in them but some nets made of palm-tree fibers and harpoons made of bone. Columbus forbade his men touching any of these things.

Cuba was the most beautiful of all the islands that had yet been discovered. The lofty trees were covered with a fine foliage, laden with beautiful blossoms or fruit, and peopled with birds of brilliant hue. Columbus did not doubt that the sweet odors filling the air came from spice trees. He believed that there were gold mines in the interior and that the oysters which he saw in the water bore pearls.

The admiral coasted along the shore of Cuba, uncertain whether it was the island of Japan or the mainland of China. He visited a village, but the terrified people fled to the mountains. The houses at this place were better built than any Indian cabins he had seen before, and he found in them rude wood carvings and masks. Columbus, ever hopeful, now felt sure that he would soon discover signs of a more advanced civilization, and believed that he was nearing an important kingdom. These people, he fancied, might prove to be tribes of poor fishermen living on the coast and selling their fish at cities in the interior. He presently found what he took to be skulls of cows, which proved to his satisfaction that there were cattle in Cuba, but they were in reality the skulls of what is known as the sea cow.

The Spaniards reached at length a large cape which was covered with palms. Three of the San Salvador Indians told Pinzon that behind this cape was a river which led to a country called Cuba-nacan, where there was much gold. In their language Cuba-nacan meant middle Cuba, *nacan* meaning middle; but Pinzon was certain that Cuba-nacan was Kublai Khan, the Emperor of China. If this were true this beautiful country would prove to be not Japan, but the mainland of China. The Spaniards set out to look for the river beyond the cape; but there was no river there, and contrary winds set in so that the ships had to turn back.

It was now the 1st of November. Columbus sent some men ashore to see the natives; but the Indians ran away as soon as the white men landed. When the Spaniards returned to their boats, the natives came back and stared at them from the shore. Columbus, who had learned his Marco Polo pretty well by heart, remembered that the Grand Khan was in the habit of sending ships to capture the natives of the islands for slaves. No doubt this was one of the islands visited by the slave ships of the Khan, and hence the reason for the alarm of the natives at the sight of vessels. With this idea in his head, Columbus sent one of his Indians ashore in a boat, charging him to tell the natives that the Spaniards were peaceable and that they had nothing to do with the Grand Khan. As the Indian interpreter knew nothing of the Grand Khan, and little of the Spanish tongue, he probably said that the white men were good people and very generous in giving away some very desirable articles, such as beads and bells. At any rate, he made a speech to the natives from the ship's boats, and then jumped out and swam ashore. Before night, sixteen canoes came out to the ships. The Indians brought cotton yarn and other such things to trade; but Columbus forbade trading for anything except gold, thinking he could in this way make the Indians bring out their hidden treasures. They really had nothing of value, however, except a silver nose ornament which one of them wore. These people said that their king lived inland, and that they had sent messengers to him to let him know of the presence of the white men.

Columbus thought that this must be some petty monarch, so he concluded to send messengers himself to find out how rich he was, and what he knew about the Grand Khan. He sent one Spaniard, one converted Jew, and two Indians on this errand. The Jew was sent because he could speak Hebrew, and some other Eastern tongues. As Columbus believed that he was on the coast of Asia, he thought it likely that the Jew would be able to talk with the king of this country. The messengers were to ask the distance to certain seaports in Asia, and were to show cinnamon, nutmegs, cloves, peppers, rhubarb, and so forth, to the king, and find out if these things grew here.

Columbus had his ships careened and calked while he was waiting for his messengers to return. He showed the Indians who hung around him gold and pearls. They used the word *bohio*, and sometimes *babeque*, when they saw gold. Some old fellows told Columbus that there was a country where the people wore such things in their ears and around their necks. They also told about people who had one eye, and others who had dogs' heads. Perhaps they believed these tales themselves, but it is also possible that they only wished to give the white men some stories large enough to suit them, or that they were speaking figuratively, after the manner of Indians, and were misunderstood.

Meantime, the town of the inland king, where the messengers had gone, proved to be an Indian village of some fifty houses. The white men were received with every honor, and seated on some curious reclining chairs in the shape of hammocks, carved to look like animals with short legs and a flattened tail. The tail was curved upward to serve as a back, and the eyes and ears were incrusted with gold.

The visitors were fed on fruits and vegetables, and their hands and feet were kissed by the men and women of the place. But the people of the village spoke neither Hebrew, Arabic, Coptic, nor Armenian, and so one of the Indian interpreters had to make a speech, in which he told them among other things that the white men had come from heaven.

As there was nothing to be learned here concerning the whereabouts of the Emperor of China, the Spaniard,

CHAIR SUCH AS COLUMBUS'S MESSENGERS SAT IN, FOUND IN A CAVE ON TURK'S ISLAND.

the Jew, and the two Indians set out on their return journey. On their way back they met Indians carrying firebrands with them, so that they might light fires with which to cook a certain root. This root was nothing less than the potato, and this was the first time that a white man saw it. The potato was destined to be worth more to Europe than all the spices for which Columbus was looking, but of course the Spaniards did not suspect this. These messengers also saw Indians rolling up dry leaves within a dry leaf, and then lighting one end of the roll and sucking the smoke into their mouths. The Indians called these rolls of dried leaves tobaccos. The innocent white man could not imagine why the Indians smoked these leaves, unless it were to perfume themselves. The same messengers were the first Europeans who saw fields of Indian corn; they also saw fields planted with potatoes, others with the yucca, the root of which was made into cassava bread, besides fields of cotton, which the Indians spun and made into hammocks or wove into a sort of apron, which the women sometimes wore.

Though the white men had discovered so much that was new and wonderful, Columbus could not find that he was any nearer the Eastern cities for which he was looking. So, taking some of the natives of Cuba with him, he set out in search of the land of *Bohio* or *Babeque*, which the Indians seemed to speak of as the land of gold.

CHAPTER XIII.

THE DISCOVERY OF HAYTI.

1492.

TROUBLED by contrary winds, Columbus did not make any new discoveries for some days. He beat about in sight of the island of Isabella, but feared to touch here lest he should lose his Indian guides, who did not like being kidnaped by the white men. The poor fellows kept a wistful eye toward San Salvador, which was their home. Meantime Pinzon thought he would try a little voyage on his own account. The Spaniards were all greedy for gold. One of the Indians on board Pinzon's ship had made him believe that he could guide him to a land of great riches. Columbus had signaled to the Pinta to join him, but she worked gradually away, and by another morning she was out of sight. This made Columbus angry, for it was the duty of Pinzon to obey him, as the admiral of the fleet. Columbus now returned to Cuba, and did some more sailing along its coasts. He found in one of the Indian cabins a cake of wax, which he took as a present to the king and queen, "for where there is wax," he said, "there must be a thousand other good things." He finally reached the eastern end of Cuba, which he thought to be the eastern end of Asia, though he called it India, for the different parts of Asia were very much mixed in people's minds in those days. Columbus did not know which way to turn. As he was sailing about in uncertainty, he saw land to the southeast. The Indians said "*Bohio*" when they saw this land, and, as Columbus thought that *bohio* meant a land where there was much gold, he steered for it. The word *bohio* is still used in Santo Domingo for a cabin, and no doubt the simple guides meant that there were many cabins here. Columbus saw that he was coming to a beautiful shore, with high mountains, rich plains, and everywhere grand tropical forests. At night, the Spaniards could see many fires, while in the day-time numerous columns of smoke rose from the land, and there seemed to be many cultivated fields. They coasted along the northern shore of the island, for this was the island of Hayti, or Santo Domingo, as we call it to-day. There were noble mountains, covered with forests of the most valuable trees, and between them lay beautiful savannas, where there were fields of grain growing, decorated here and there with palms. There were so many fish in the sea that they sometimes jumped into the Spaniards' boats, and the voyagers heard what they thought to be the song of the nightingale in the woods, though there are no nightingales in America.

The island of Hayti seemed to Columbus the most beautiful of all; he therefore named it for Spain, Hispaniola. When the white men landed, they found that the people had all fled. As Columbus could see cultivated fields, he thought that the people of Hispaniola were perhaps more civilized than the other Indians that he had found. Columbus set up a cross to show that he took possession of the country. Three sailors, who wandered about in the woods while this ceremony was being performed, happened on a crowd of Indians, who ran away very fast, not being troubled with any clothes to hinder them. The sailors ran after them and caught one young woman, whom they took back to the ships.

"SHE MAY NOT HAVE ENJOYED THE CLOTHING VERY MUCH."

As she wore no clothing whatever, it was necessary to give up the theory that the natives of Hayti might be more civilized than those of other islands; but, on the other hand, the young woman, not to be wholly without decoration, wore a gold ornament in her nose, which gave the Spaniards encouragement. Columbus caused the woman to be clad, presented her with some trifles, and then set her free. In that warm climate this young savage may not have enjoyed the clothing very much, but she was no doubt delighted with her beads and bells.

The next day the admiral sent some men and a Cuban Indian on shore to see if they could not get a chance to talk with the people of the village from which the woman had come. The messengers, after walking a considerable distance, found a large Indian village in a beautiful valley on the shores of a river. Here were banana and palm trees, with birds gayly singing among the branches, though it was now December. There were a thousand houses in this town, but people there were none; all had taken flight. The Cuban Indian was sent in pursuit of them. They were not so much afraid of a naked man of their own color, so they let him come near, and listened while he persuaded them to return and see the visitors from the skies. The Indians after a while ventured slowly back, stopping every now and then to put their hands on their heads, which was either an act of politeness with them or some charm to keep them from harm at the hands of these strange beings. A second company of Indians arrived soon after, carrying the woman whom the Spaniards had clothed upon their shoulders, to show how pleased they were with the treatment she had received. The savages gave the white men food and whatever else they required. They wished them to stay in their village all night, but the messengers returned to the ships. They told Columbus that they had seen a very rich and beautiful country, and that the people were finer looking and lighter colored than the Indians they had seen in the other islands.

Columbus prosecuted his voyage still farther along the northern coast of Hayti. One night, when he was in the channel between the islands of Tortuga and Hispaniola, he came upon an Indian paddling alone in a canoe. He wondered that a man should venture so far from land when the wind was blowing hard and the sea was rough. He did not see how the fellow could keep his tiny boat from turning over. The Spaniards picked up this solitary navigator, took his canoe in tow, fed him with sweets, decked him with beads and hawkbells, and then sent him ashore on the island of Hispaniola. When the Indian told his friends how well he had been treated, they soon came out to the ships with their usual merchandise to trade for gewgaws. They wore some gold ornaments, which gave the Spaniards new hopes.

The signs of gold increased. One chief was found who cut a plate of gold as large as his hand into pieces and traded it with the white men. He promised to bring more gold the following day. The next day some sailors, who had been ashore, hastened on board to tell Columbus that this king was coming to see him; not on foot, however, though he was a young man, but carried on a sort of hand-barrow or litter, by four men. When he arrived, Columbus was eating his dinner in the cabin. He ordered the monarch of the hand-barrow to be brought to him. The king entered the cabin of Columbus, commanding his followers with a wave of the hand to stay outside, which they did, squatting on the deck, except two old men, who entered with the king and sat at his feet. Columbus, always ready to apply European notions to America, conjectured that one of these men was the king's tutor and the other his counselor. This savage monarch would not permit the admiral to rise from his dinner, so Columbus caused some of his dishes to be offered to the chief. The latter tasted each dish very daintily, and then turned it over to the tutor and counselor, who devoured it quickly enough. He did the same with the drinks that were offered him, and Columbus was charmed with his air of stately dignity. He spoke little, but Columbus was sure that what he said must be very judicious, though he did

The Indian monarch and his councillors visit Columbus.

not understand a word of it. After dinner was over, one of the officers of this king brought a belt, which the white men thought almost as fine as a Spanish belt, though of a different workmanship. This is the first time in history that we hear of the wampum belt, which Indian chiefs used in making a friendly treaty. It is strange that these island chiefs should have had the same custom as our North American Indians.

The king gave the admiral the belt and two very tiny morsels of worked gold. Seeing that his guest admired the cover of his bed very much, Columbus took it off and made him a present of it. He also gave him several amber beads, which he wore around his own neck, some red shoes, and a bottle of orange water. The king was very much delighted and astonished with the scent of the orange water. The admiral thought he said that he was sorry that they could not understand each other, and that he was the king of the whole island. Columbus showed him a gold ducat with the heads of Ferdinand and Isabella stamped on it, and some royal banners. The king remarked that these monarchs no doubt lived in the heavens. He was sent ashore in the ship's boat, with every honor, for Columbus was impressed with the dignity of a king who made his journeys on a hand-barrow. Having reached the shore, the chief once more mounted his litter, while one of his sons was carried behind him on the shoulder of an Indian subject. Perhaps this was the crown prince.

CHAPTER XIV.

WRECKED.

1492.

It was Christmas eve. The sea was as calm as the water in a porringer, to use the words of Columbus. The admiral had not slept for two days and a night, so he left the helm in the hands of an experienced pilot and went to bed about eleven o'clock. Columbus was no sooner asleep than the helmsman turned the rudder over to a boy, and went to sleep himself. Meantime the currents drew the ship slowly toward a sand bank. She touched so softly that there was almost no shock. The boy who was steering felt the helm stop and heard the breakers on the sand bar. He began to cry out. Columbus was on his feet in an instant, and was the first man on deck. The pilot and several sailors ran out next. Columbus ordered them to get into the boat and throw out an anchor astern in order to warp the ship off. Instead of doing this the cowards rowed for the Nina, which was half a league away.

Meantime the current was driving the ship farther and farther on the bar. Columbus had her mast cut away, hoping that this would lighten her so that she would float once more. But it did no good. The vessel settled on her side, and her seams began to open. The men on the Nina would have nothing to do with the

WRECKED. 83

runaway sailors, so they presently came back to their own ship, when it was too late to be of any service.

SHIPWRECK.

There was nothing for the crew to do but to take refuge in the Nina. Two officers were sent on shore to tell the king of this part of the island of the misfortunes that had befallen the white men. This chief heard the sad story with tears, and sent a number of Indians with their canoes to help the Spaniards save the ship's cargo. The chief, whose name was Guacanagari, presently came out in a canoe himself, and politely watched to see that his men did their best in helping the whites. Every now and then the Indian king is said to have sent some relative of his to visit Columbus, and tell him with tears, not to afflict himself, for Guacanagari would give him all that he possessed. The kindness of this chief was real, for there was not a pin missing of the cargo when it was got together on shore, where the chief set some of his warriors to stand guard over it. But in spite of the friendliness of these simple people, Columbus did not spend a merry Christmas.

Guacanagari made the admiral a visit on board the Nina the day after Christmas, showing his sympathy by a very sad face. He offered Columbus anything that he had, and said that he had already set apart three houses to store his goods in. While they were talking, a canoe load of strange Indians appeared on the scene, bringing leaves of gold to exchange for little bells. The sailors, too, who had been ashore in the village of Guacanagari, also said that the Indians had given them gold for the smallest trifles. The face of Columbus lighted up at this news. The Indian chief was quick to see this, and told Columbus something about a place called Cibao, where there was much gold. He said that he would have plenty of gold brought from there as soon as possible. Columbus had heard the Indians mention Cibao before in connection with gold, and he

WRECKED.

jumped to the conclusion that it meant Cipango, or Japan.

Guacanagari invited Columbus to go ashore and eat with him, and the invitation was accepted. The feast consisted of coneys or little rabbits, fish, fruits, and cassava bread. The white men had not learned to like the Indian food yet, and preferred their own salt meat, sea biscuits, and wine. The king ate very slowly, washed his hands when done, and rubbed them with scented herbs. The chief ended the day's entertainment by giving Columbus a sort of carved mask, with eyes and ears of gold, and some necklaces, from which hung gold plates.

AN INDIAN MASK FROM HAYTI.

Columbus now began to imagine it a lucky accident which had wrecked him on this coast, where there was so much promise of gold. His men were having a very good time on shore, with no work to do and plenty of tropical food to eat. Some of them proposed to stay on the island while Columbus returned to Spain, for the Nina was not large enough to carry them all. This idea pleased the admiral greatly. He resolved to have a little fort built out of the wrecked ship, and to leave a colony in Hispaniola.

While the fort was building, Columbus dwelt in the largest house in the Indian village. This house was carpeted with palm leaves. Whenever Guacanagari came to see the admiral, he hung some gold ornaments around his neck. Columbus in return gave the chief necklaces of green beads, a mantle of fine cloth, a pair of colored boots, and a large silver finger ring. Guacanagari told Columbus about his troubles, which consisted mainly in a lively dread of the natives of the Caribbee Islands, who came and carried off the people of Hispaniola as captives. Columbus promised the chief that the Spaniards would protect them from the Caribs, though he had not the least idea who the Caribs were, or where they came from. Before leaving, Columbus thought best, for more reasons than one, to show Guacanagari the power of the white men, so he sent to the Nina for a Moorish bow and arrows, together with a certain Spaniard who was a very good marksman. The Indians were much pleased with this man's skill. An arquebus, which was the clumsy gun of that day, was also discharged, and a sort of cannon called a Lombard was fired into the hull of the wrecked ship. The fire-arms were too much for the Indians. King and subjects fell on the ground at the first report. They were much frightened, but when they were assured that these weapons should be used against their enemies, the Caribs, their fright is said to have changed to delight.

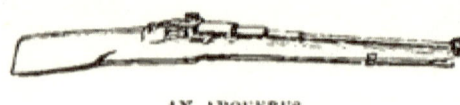

AN ARQUEBUS.

The admiral left his little colony all the trinkets there were on board the two vessels, with which to trade, as well as provisions, arms, tools, seeds, cannon and powder, and a ship's boat. He expected when he came back to find a ton of gold gathered by trading with the Indians. He left thirty-nine men at this colony.

As a part of the seamen who sailed with Columbus were released prisoners, it is likely that many of the men who consented to remain behind were criminals who had their own reasons for not caring to go home. This was a very bad seed to sow in a new soil. Columbus named his fort La Navidad, or the Nativity, because he had been wrecked here on Christmas eve.

A LOMBARD.

CHAPTER XV.

A SKIRMISH.

1493.

On the 4th day of January, 1493, the Nina was towed out of the harbor of La Navidad, and made her start for Spain. The wind was contrary, and she pushed slowly along the northern coast of Hispaniola. One day, while the Nina was beating about in sight of a bold mountain-peak which Columbus named Monte Christo, a sailor who was on the lookout called from the mast where he was perched that the Pinta was in sight. The men on the Nina were overjoyed, for they dreaded to take the long voyage to Spain alone in their indifferent little ship. Pinzon made some very poor excuses to the admiral for his long absence. But Columbus dared not reprove him, for he had many relatives and friends in the two ships, and Columbus did not want anything to happen to hinder him from getting back to Spain safely with his good news. Pinzon had really gone off on a voyage of his own. He had wasted some time cruising about among small islands, and had then gone to Hispaniola and traded for gold along the coast. Half of this gold he kept, and gave the other half to his sailors to persuade them to conceal the fact, for the gold belonged to the crown. The thrifty Pinzon had also captured four Indian men and two girls, whom he meant to sell in Spain for slaves.

A SKIRMISH.

The weather was still rough after the Pinta had joined the Nina, so that Columbus was detained some time longer off the coast of Hispaniola. He saw here what he thought to be mermaids, for people at that time believed in the existence of these beauties of the sea. But Columbus did not find them so beautiful as they had been represented, for the mermaids of Columbus

COLUMBUS FINDS MERMAIDS LESS BEAUTIFUL THAN THEY HAD BEEN REPRESENTED TO BE.

were probably sea calves. The ships presently came to the river where Pinzon had been trading. Columbus made his rebellious captain put ashore the men and girls that he had captured for slaves, for he did not wish the Indians to have any reason to hate the Spaniards. The ships at length reached the great bay of Samana, on the western end of the island, and the admiral sent some of his men to the land to fill the water casks for the long voyage, for this was to be the last stopping-place before sailing for Spain.

The men were met by a number of Indians armed with bows and arrows, tipped with fish teeth, and carrying heavy wooden swords or clubs with which they could break a man's skull. They were painted, and resembled in all points a party of our North America Indians on the war-path. They did not fight the white men at this time, however, but sold some of their bows and arrows to the sailors. Columbus concluded that these fierce braves must be the Caribs of whom the other Indians seemed so much afraid, for he believed that the natives whom he had seen hitherto were always as gentle and friendly as they appeared.

One naked warrior came on board the Nina. Columbus talked with him by signs and by the aid of a San Salvador Indian, and got some prodigious lies for his pains. When asked where the country of the Caribs was, the Indian pointed to the east and added the information that in that country gold was found in pieces half as large as the poop of the Nina. Columbus also got from him some story about an island which was peopled only by women. It is likely that he was looking for such a place, for Marco Polo told about an island near Asia where women lived alone, and another one where only men lived, and the discoverer was always on the lookout for these places. Columbus fed the Indian, gave him a bead necklace and some colored stuffs, and set him ashore to tell his people to bring any gold they might have to the ships.

The seven Spaniards who took the Indians ashore began to trade with the natives they found there. These fellows, however, presently seized their bows and arrows, as well as some cords for tying prisoners, and began to fight. The Spaniards immediately fell upon them, and wounded one in the breast with an arrow and another in the back with a sword. The courage of the Indians departed quickly; they fled to the woods, dropping their arms by the way. Columbus regretted this skirmish, but reflected that it might have a good effect in making the natives afraid to attack the little colony he had left behind. The Indians took it all in good part, however, and their chief sent Columbus a string of beads made of shells, that is to say, what in North America is called a wampum belt. The Indians began to come on board, and four young fellows, probably wishing to be rid of the new comers, told him some tales of an island lying to the eastward. They were carried off for their pains, for Columbus insisted that they should go to the island with him as guides. As the island did not appear and the wind was favorable, the ships bore away for Spain and the Indians had to make the rough voyage with them.

A WAMPUM BELT.

CHAPTER XVI.

THE RETURN VOYAGE.
1493.

The Pinta and the Nina were both very leaky, and the sailors had to work hard to keep down the water. But they had a good wind, and the ships sped swiftly along toward the Old World. The men caught some tunny-fish and killed a shark, which they were glad to eat, for their supplies were running low and all they had left was sea biscuit, wine, and some agi-peppers, which they had brought with them from the West Indies. They made such good progress that in less than a month all hands began to look for Spain, or at least for the Canaries.

But on the 12th of February there came up a violent wind, and the sea ran very high. On the next day, toward night, the wind increased and there were flashes of lightning in the northeast. Columbus predicted a storm, and it did not delay. The two leaky little ships scudded along all night under bare poles. Neither of them had decks, and they must have been very uncomfortable places in a wintry gale. The storm let up a little on the morning of the 14th, and the ships made some sail, but the wind presently came up from the south more furiously than ever. The men had to take in sail and let the ships drive before the hurricane. Darkness came on once more, and the vessels signaled to one another with lights. For a long while the men on the Nina could see the lights of the Pinta, but presently they were lost in the tempest. When morning came there was no ship to be seen, and the despairing men on the Nina gave her up for lost, and expected that their turn would come next.

As the day wore on, the storm increased in violence. There seemed to be no hope for the men on the little Nina unless Heaven should come to their help, and so they made vows after the custom of their time. Columbus caused as many beans as there were men on the ship to be put into a cup. On one of these beans was cut a cross. Every one then made a vow that should he draw the marked bean, he would, if the ship got safe to land, make a pilgrimage to the shrine of St. Mary of Guadaloupe, carrying a wax candle weighing five pounds. Columbus drew the bean with the cross on it. The beans were put in a cup again, and this time another pilgrimage was vowed. A sailor drew the marked bean, and Columbus promised to give him money with which to pay the expenses of his pilgrimage. Another lot was then cast for a pilgrimage to still another shrine, to say a mass there and watch all night in the chapel. Columbus again drew the marked bean. As the storm grew worse than ever, sailors, officers, and men at once made a solemn vow that were they ever spared to reach land, they would go, barefooted and clad only in their shirts, in procession to the nearest church dedicated to the Virgin to give thanks.

After making their vows, the sailors bethought themselves to fill all the empty barrels with sea water, for the ship lacked ballast, because so much of the water and food had been used on the voyage that she rolled very badly. Still matters grew worse and worse. The

COLUMBUS AND THE SAILORS DRAW BEANS.

men cursed their admiral for having taken them into such dangers, and for not having turned back, as they had desired him on many occasions. The unhappy Columbus knew very well that he had made a great discovery, which would make his name known for all time if he could once reach Spain with the news of it. Now, however, the very memory of his achievement was about to be swallowed up in the ocean, and in time to come sailors would forever be afraid to follow in his track, imagining that he had come to some mysterious and dreadful end. Then he thought about his two little boys, Diego and Ferdinand, at school in Cordova. Their father lost, the king and queen would never know the great service that he had rendered them, so that there would be no one to befriend the children. In his sad thoughts Columbus imagined that he was now to be terribly punished for his sins by being deprived of the glory of his great success. Then he began to wonder if there were not some way in which, though he should be dead and the ship lost with every soul on board, the news of his discovery might yet be saved.

Having thought of a plan, he sat down amid all this confusion of the elements and wrote on parchment how he had found the land that he had gone to seek, and promised to discover, how many days it had taken to sail there, and by what route he had sailed, as well as a description of the country and the people. Columbus sealed his parchment and addressed it to the king and queen of Spain, writing on the outside that he who would deliver it should have a reward of a thousand ducats. He then wrapped the parchment in a waxed cloth and put it into an empty barrel, which he caused to be carefully headed and thrown into the sea. He did not tell his men what this was for, but let them think that he was performing some vow. His mind was still uneasy lest the barrel should never reach land,

96   THE STORY OF COLUMBUS.

which, in fact, it never did, so far as is known. So he wrote another account, sealed it in the same way, and put it in an empty cask, which he placed on the high poop of his ship, so that should she go down, the barrel would float off and stand a chance of being picked up.

COLUMBUS WRITES AN ACCOUNT OF HIS DISCOVERY.

CHAPTER XVII.

LAND.

1493.

On the morning of the 15th of February a sailor who was on the lookout in the rigging gave the cry of land. The men were wild with delight. No one knew what the land was. Some thought it the island of Madeira, some Portugal, and some Spain, but Columbus believed it to be one of the Azores. The storm was so great that for two days the ship beat about in sight of land, unable to make it. Once she threw out an anchor, but her cable broke. Finally she anchored under shelter of the northern shore of the island. Columbus had scarcely eaten or slept for many days. He now took a little rest and awoke suffering with the gout.

The island proved to be St. Mary, the most southern of the Azores. The people of the island were astonished that the Nina had outlived such a storm. They were wonder-struck when they heard of the discoveries that had been made, but the governor of the island had his own opinion about it. He made no doubt that Columbus had been interfering with some of the discoveries of the crown of Portugal, to which this island belonged. Nevertheless, he sent polite messages to the Spanish admiral, together with bread, fowls, and other fresh provisions. Columbus had not forgotten the vow that he and his men had made, so he asked if there was any church on the island dedicated to the Virgin Mary. He was told that there was a small hermitage, built on the rocks behind the next point. Columbus asked the men who had come out to the ship to find the priest who had the key to the little chapel, and have it un-

SHORE OF THE AZORES.

locked. The next day he reminded his men of their vow. It was agreed that half of them should go barefoot and in their shirts to the little church on the rocks, and that when they returned the other half should do the same. The sailors went, but the day wore on and they did not return. Columbus began to be uneasy. A point hid the chapel from view. He changed the anchorage of the Nina, so that he could see the hermitage. There were a number of armed men on horseback on the shore. Columbus saw them get into the ship's boat and row out toward the vessel.

The fact was that the governor of St. Mary had taken the sailors prisoners in their rather scanty costume, while they were performing their vow. The Portuguese, having been almost the only discoverers of new lands up to this time, were naturally jealous that Spain should enter the field as a rival. The governor of the island came out to the Nina in the captured ship's boat. Both he and Columbus talked very boastfully as officers of their different crowns, and Columbus swore that if his men were not delivered up he would carry a hundred of the inhabitants of St. Mary captive to Spain; but they came to no settlement.

In spite of the way in which he had spoken to the governor, Columbus was anxious. Perhaps war had broken out between Spain and Portugal while he was away. He moved back to his first anchorage, so that the ship would not get the force of the waves so much. The next day the weather was bad, and Columbus had to sail over toward the island of St. Michael and take shelter behind it. He had a great deal of trouble to manage his ship, for there were only three old hands left on board, the rest being landsmen and Indians, which last were of no account whatever. Columbus had to do a sailor's work himself. The vessel got through the night safely, and as the storm had abated the next day, Columbus returned to St. Mary toward evening. The ship's boat came out from the island again, bringing a notary. Having first been assured of his safety, the notary got aboard the Nina, where he spent the night. He was very polite, and said that the governor only wished to know whether the admiral had a commission from the King and Queen of Spain. Columbus was equally polite, and showed his papers. The notary went away satisfied, and presently the sailors all came back in the ship's boat.

In consequence of this bad reception at the Azores and the roughness of the weather, Columbus did not get a chance to take in the ballast which his ship needed. He weighed anchor, and the wind blew the Nina toward Spain, but quite too furiously. At one time a dove lit on the ship, and again the men saw many little birds that had been driven out to sea by the storm. The tempest increased. On the 3d of March the Spaniards furled their sails and began to despair once more of ever reaching Spain. This time they made a vow and drew lots that one of their number should go barefoot and in his shirt to a certain church in Huelva, the marked bean falling to Columbus once more.

The Nina rushed along under a furious gale, without an inch of sail, and with the sea running to a terrific height, while there were lightning flashes and bursts of thunder. Columbus felt as though he were repulsed "from the very door of the house," as he said. In the middle of the night came the cry of land, but this only added to the terror of the seamen, for the ship was in danger of being driven ashore headlong and wrecked. In order to prevent this, they managed to make a little sail. When morning came, Columbus saw that he was off the point of Cintra, near the city of Lisbon, in Portugal. There was nothing for it but to take refuge in the harbor, and brave the Portuguese in their very capital.

The Nina had no sooner entered the bay than the people ran in crowds to look at her, as though they were gazing on a miracle. They were, in truth, astonished that so frail a bark had weathered the storm when

PORT OF LISBON.

there was news everywhere of wrecks. Columbus sent a courier to the King and Queen of Spain with the news of his discovery. He also wrote to the King of Portugal, telling him where he had been, and asking that he might enter the port of Lisbon. He did this because the story had got about that his ship was loaded with gold, and he was afraid of being troubled.

The captain of a Portuguese man-of-war which lay near him summoned Columbus on board his vessel to account for himself. But Columbus stood upon his dignity as a Spanish admiral, and refused to come. When the Portuguese captain heard, however, what an extraordinary voyage the Nina had been on, he came to visit Columbus with the music of drums, fifes, and trumpets.

By the next day the water was covered with boat-loads of people who had come out to see the Indians on board the Nina, and hear the sailors tell of the strange lands to which they had been. The king gave orders that Columbus should have everything given to him of which he had need. He also asked the discoverer to come and see him in his palace at Valparaiso. So Columbus went to see King John of Portugal once more. He was received with every honor. The king made him put on his hat again when he had taken it off in his presence, and seated him by his side as though he were a royal personage. He made Columbus tell him all about his voyage. The kings of Portugal were intelligent men and much interested in discoveries by sea. King John could not but admire so brave a deed, but he regretted sorely that he had not undertaken this voyage himself. He remarked that he was not sure whether, according to the treaty he had made with Spain, he might not lay claim to this new country. Portugal had indeed a papal grant to all the lands discovered from Cape Non, in Africa, to the Indies. If Columbus had found the Indies, he might be interfering with the rights of Portugal. Columbus said that he did not know anything about the treaty, but that the King and Queen of Spain had ordered him not to go near the coast of Africa, and that he had obeyed them. The king answered politely that it was all right, and that no doubt there would be no trouble about it. After the discoverer had visited the king, he had to visit the queen and tell her about his adventures.

On the 13th of March Columbus made sail for Spain, and after two days he anchored in the harbor of Palos, out of which he had sailed seven months and a half before. The people of Palos were wild with delight. They came to meet him in procession, shouting with excitement. They held it a great honor that Columbus had sailed from their town, priding themselves on it as much as though they had not done their utmost to defeat his enterprise at the outset.

CHAPTER XVIII.

REJOICINGS AT COURT.

1492.

The Pinta had not foundered, as Columbus supposed. Those on board of her did not doubt, in their turn, that the Nina was lost, and Martin Alonzo Pinzon thought to be the first to carry the good news to Spain and to gain much of the credit that was due to Columbus. The Pinta made land in Galicia, and Pinzon hastened to send his account of the new discoveries to Ferdinand and Isabella, and to ask for permission to come to court. The king and queen had perhaps heard already of the behavior of Pinzon in the West Indies, for Co-

ROYAL PALACE, BARCELONA.

REJOICINGS AT COURT.

lumbus had sent a courier to them from Portugal. They sent Pinzon word that they would not see him unless he came in the suite of Columbus, where he belonged. Pinzon came back to Palos ill the same day that Columbus reached there, and died soon after. Some writers say that he died of a broken heart because of the refusal of the king and queen to see him.

Ferdinand and Isabella sent for Columbus to come to court, which was then at Barcelona. So the navigator set out, carrying with him the gold he had brought and the curiosities of the West Indies, among which were six Indians. One of the Indians that Columbus had brought with him had died on the voyage and three were left sick at Palos, for Indians do not readily stand changes of place and new modes of living. The great discoverer traveled very slowly, because he was stopped on the road by crowds of people who thronged around him to stare at the Indians and ask questions about the voyage. He reached Barcelona about the middle of April, a month after he had landed. Meantime, Ferdinand and Isabella, highly delighted with the success of the enterprise, had ordered that a grand reception should be prepared for Columbus. The courtiers went out to meet him, and there was a great procession through the city in sight of the multitudes that filled the streets and crowded the windows and housetops to get a look at Columbus and his wild men from the New World.

The king and queen seated themselves on a throne, beneath a canopy of gold brocade, with their son, Prince Juan, beside them, to receive the great discoverer. Columbus knelt to kiss the hands of their majesties, but they raised him up and caused him to sit down in their presence, which was a great honor in a land of severe etiquette like Spain. The monarchs then bade Columbus tell them all about his voyage, and made him show them the parrots, strange plants, ornaments of gold, and the natives that he had brought with him. This done, Ferdinand and Isabella fell on their knees and gave thanks to God for the wonderful discovery. When all was over, the admiral was conducted to his lodgings by the courtiers in procession. After this, when the king rode out, Columbus rode on one side of him and the crown prince on the other, which was the greatest compliment that could have been paid the discoverer.

The pension promised to the first man who should see land was granted to Columbus, who saw the trembling light on the eve of his great discovery. The admiral has been much criticized for taking this pension away from a poor sailor. It is not known for what reasons the discoverer was preferred to the seaman of the Pinta. It should be remembered, however, that the captain and the crew of this ship were in disgrace for having deserted the admiral, and plotted to rob the government of the much desired gold.

The news of the discovery traveled fast. It was soon known in the courts of Europe and discussed by learned men. The letter Columbus had sent to Ferdinand and Isabella from his ship, was printed in different places. In the court of Henry VII. of England, men said that it was a thing "more divine than human."

Everybody believed, as Columbus did, that he had found a way to the most eastern parts of Asia, and it took a long time to get this notion out of men's heads.

This belief caused the new islands to be known as the Indies, and after a while as the West Indies, while the name of the Antilles came from the tradition of an island called Antilla in the Atlantic Ocean. It was also because of the belief that India had been found that natives of the New World were called Indians.

The Pope was supposed to have a right to grant heathen lands to Christian kings, so Ferdinand and Isabella hastened to send him the news of the great discovery, and ask him to give them a right to the lands which Columbus had found for them. He did this, and,

CADIZ, FROM THE MOLE.

as the Portuguese were jealous that the Spanish discoveries might interfere with theirs, the Pope established an imaginary line in the Atlantic Ocean, from north to south, giving Spain all the land on the west of this line, and Portugal all the land found on the east.

Great haste was made to send out a second fleet to the new world to make sure of the discoveries. Juan Rodriguez de Fonseca, archdeacon of Seville and after-

SEVILLE.

ward a bishop, was given control of India affairs, as they were called, with an office at Seville. Fonseca and Columbus were very busy getting ready for the new voyage. Seventeen ships, little and big, were to sail this time from Cadiz, and it took a great deal of money to pay the expenses of so great a fleet. Part of the funds came from the sale of the gold and jewels taken from the unhappy Jews whom Ferdinand and Isabella had driven from Spain, for it was thought in those days a religious act to persecute all who did not believe in Christianity.

The arms which the men who went on this new voyage were to carry came from the beautiful Moorish palace of the Alhambra, which was at this time used as an arsenal. In those days gunpowder was not yet much employed in light warfare. The arquebuse, which was the hand gun of that day, was heavy and awkward, for the man who used it had to carry a stand with him to rest it on when he fired, and soldiers naturally prefered the bow and arrow.

Queen Isabella interested herself very much in plans for converting the Indians. The six natives whom Columbus had brought to Barcelona were baptized, the king, queen, and Prince Juan being sponsors. Prince Juan chose one of these Indians to add to his attendants. The poor fellow died some two years afterward, as these people almost always did when removed from their home, and the Spaniards pleased themselves with the thought that he was the first of these wild people to enter heaven.

CHAPTER XIX.

THE SECOND VOYAGE.

1493.

THOSE who went with Columbus on his first voyage thought that they were doomed men. The second expedition was quite another affair. It was said that men were almost willing to jump into the sea and swim to these new lands. The magic word gold had been spoken, and thousands, many of whom were of the nobility,

THE HARBOR, LOOKING FROM CADIZ.

flocked to Columbus to beg employment in the new colony. People thought they had only to go to the Indies to pick up gold. The voyage also seemed to offer a fine field for adventure, better even than had the Moorish wars. Many had to be refused, and as it was, more were engaged to go than had been intended.

Columbus bids good-by to his sons.

THE SECOND VOYAGE.   111

Among others who were to sail with Columbus was his younger brother Diego, who had no doubt come from Genoa as soon as he had heard of the good fortune of Christopher.

Horses were put on the ships, as well as cattle, seeds, vines, sugar-canes, and grafts. Besides these things, the vessels were loaded with an abundance of beads, hawksbells, looking-glasses, and such other inexpensive trinkets as would take the fancy of the Indians.

There was so much to be done that the fleet could not be got ready to sail until the 25th of September, 1493. There was a great bustle of departure and leave-taking in the harbor of Cadiz an hour before sunrise on the morning of the sailing, for fifteen hundred people, many of them men of high rank, were starting out for the New World, and crowds had come to bid them farewell. Among the others gathered there in the early morning were the sons of Columbus, come to see their father off. The great discoverer was very fond of these two boys. One of the purposes of his life was to make them great and rich men.

The ships were finally off. They made sail for the Canaries, where they stopped some time, laying in meat, wood, and water for the voyage. While Columbus was at the Canaries he gave to each one of his captains a sealed paper, commanding them not to open the papers unless they got lost from the fleet. These papers gave directions for sailing to Hispaniola, for Columbus wished to keep the route a secret as far as possible, so that others should not get in ahead of him and reap the fruits of his enterprise.

The fleet lost sight of the last of the Canaries on the

13th of October. The weather was fine, and the ships sped along for the New World. Once, indeed, they had a violent thunder storm, and blue flames were seen rising from the tips of the masts. This was the electrical light known as St. Elmo's fire. The superstitious Spanish sailors, believing this to be St. Elmo himself, thought they were safe when they saw the flames, and began to say litanies and sing chants.

This time the fleet reached land in twenty days after leaving the Canaries. The ships had gone farther south than Columbus had sailed before, and one of the Caribbee Islands was the first land seen. The people on board shouted with joy, for they had got very tired of the bad sea food and of bailing water out of the leaky ships, and had been sighing for land for some time. Columbus named the island Dominica, which means Sunday, because he had found it on that day. Though it was the 3d of November, when everything was dull and brown in Spain, Dominica was green from the tops of her mountains to the water's edge, "which was delightful to see," in the opinion of the men on board the fleet. During this first day six islands could be seen from the ships, each beautifully green; the air was sweet with the scent of flowers, and flocks of parrots and other birds of brilliant color flew from one island to another. Columbus could find no good harbor in Dominica, so he sailed to another island, which he called Marigalante, after his ship. The admiral went ashore at Marigalante, carrying the royal banner, to take possession, and found the island was covered with dense woods, of such kinds of trees as the Spaniards had never seen before, some bearing fruit and some in blos-

THE SECOND VOYAGE. 113

som. The men found one leaf which had a promising smell of cloves, while some of them tasted an unknown fruit and were made ill by it. There seemed to be no people on this island, and Columbus only remained

MARIGALANTE ISLAND.

there two hours. The next day he sailed for another very large island. The ships ran by a high mountain on the shore of this island with a peak, which was the crater of a volcano. Streams of water ran down the mountain, and in one place there was a waterfall which seemed to come from the sky, so high was it. As the cascade fell it became clouds of foam, which looked in the distance like white rock, and the men on shipboard disputed whether it was rock or water, and made wagers with one another regarding it. Columbus named this island Guadalupe, because he had promised the monks of Our Lady of Guadalupe to name some new land for their convent. There were some small villages on the sea-shore, but the people who lived in them fled as soon as they spied a sail. The admiral sent some men ashore to find out what sort of people lived here, though the Spaniards suspected that those they had seen running were not embarrassed by clothing.

The men found the cabins much like those which Columbus had seen before—little thatched roofs, with hammocks strung from their posts, furnished with dishes made out of calabashes, or of rude earthenware; cotton spun and unspun; bows and arrows tipped with bone, and some very large, tame parrots, with plumage of green, white, blue, and red. There were also some fruits which looked like great green pine cones, but which proved to have a delicious taste. This was the first time that white men had ever tasted pine-apples. In one of the cabins was a little frightened, naked child, whom the parents had forgotten when they ran away. The Spaniards put some strings of glass beads around the arms of the child, so that when the people came back they would see that the strangers meant to be friendly. The white men found human bones about these cabins, which made Columbus think that these were the very Caribs of which other Indians were afraid, and said that they ate human flesh.

In the next few days the Spaniards captured some Indians, and some women fled to them. These women were prisoners who had been carried away from other islands, and, as the Spaniards thought, expecting to be eaten, preferred to try their chances with the white strangers. Columbus had them decorated with bells and set ashore, though the poor creatures seemed to be

An Indian child is found in a hut.

THE SECOND VOYAGE. 115

reluctant to go. The boats had no sooner put them ashore and pushed off again than their Indian masters rushed out and tore the ornaments off of them. The next day, when some men were ashore getting water, these women came and begged to be taken back, so the sailors took pity on them and took them to the ships. The Indian women told Columbus that most of the men of the place had gone off in their canoes to make captives on some of the other islands.

MAP OF COLUMBUS' SECOND VOYAGE.

CHAPTER XX.

ADVENTURES AMONG THE CARIBBEE ISLANDS.
1493.

One of the Spanish captains with eight men had gone ashore on the island of Guadalupe (or, as the present French possessors call it, Guadaloupe), without permission from the admiral, and did not return. Columbus was in haste to sail for Hispaniola. Parties went ashore and scrambled about in the thick woods, firing an arquebuse from time to time, but they found no sign of the lost Spaniards. There was nothing to do but to wait another day. So Columbus ordered that the time should be used in getting in water and wood, and washing clothes.

While the linen of fifteen hundred men fluttered in the breeze, Alonzo de Ojeda, a bold fellow, with some forty men, beat up the woods in search of the lost Spaniards, blowing trumpets and discharging guns. They returned without finding them, but said that they had discovered such valuable things as mastic, aloes, sandalwood, frankincense, and cinnamon trees, and that they had seen falcons, kites, turtle-doves, crows, partridges, and nightingales. Ojeda also said that they had waded through twenty-six rivers. It is quite likely that Ojeda waded through the windings of the same river more than once, as well as that he saw spices and birds other than those of which he boasted.

After the stragglers had been gone four days, Columbus concluded that they had been eaten by cannibals. He was about to sail when the wanderers hailed the ships from shore. They had been lost in the tropical tangle, and had scrambled about unable to find the coast. One man had climbed one of the immense trees to try to get the points of the compass by means of an observation of the stars, but the great canopy of leaves at the top concealed the sky from sight. The men had finally happened upon the shore, and so found their way to the ships, looking worn and half starved. Hungry as they were, Columbus punished them for going ashore without permission by putting them in irons on half-rations.

The Indian women on board the fleet said that there were other islands to the south of Guadaloupe, and that beyond them was the mainland, which was true, strange to say—for the white men did not usually get any very correct information from the natives. Columbus, however, anxious to reach the little colony he had left, held his course for Hispaniola. He passed many beautiful islands, and named them in passing. As the weather was bad, the fleet anchored at one which was named Santa Cruz. A well-manned barge was sent ashore, with instructions to talk with the Indians, and try to get from them directions for reaching Hispaniola. The people fled, however, and the men only found several women and children, whom they took to be prisoners of the Caribs.

While the fleet lay at anchor, a canoe came in sight with four men, two women, and two boys in it. These Indians had not seen the ships, on account of the windings of the shore, until they were quite near them. When they saw the strange sight, they stopped paddling and lay stupefied with amazement for almost an hour, within two gunshots of the vessels. The barge was just starting back from its trip to the shore, when the crew saw the wonderstruck Indians. The ship's boat altered its course, and crept slowly along shore until it had cut off retreat for the canoe. The Indians paddled with all their might when they saw the barge close upon them. But the Spaniards gained on them, and when the Caribs saw that they could not escape, they took to their bows and arrows, both men and women, and began to fight. Their aim was so good that they wounded two Spaniards, although the white men were defended by shields or wooden bucklers. The barge ran down the canoe and upset it, or the white men would soon have been all killed. These brave Indians, after their canoe was overturned, swam about in the water, wading where it was shallow enough, and taking the chance to get a fresh shot at the enemy. The Spaniards had as much as they could do to take them prisoners, and indeed they could not get one fellow until he was mortally wounded with a lance. One of the wounded Spaniards afterward died, for these Indians used poisoned arrows.

The Spaniards noticed that the costumes of the Caribs was different from that of the other Indians they had seen—that is to say, that they wore their hair longer, and, instead of decorating their faces with crosses and other figures, they stained their eyebrows and eyelids, which made them look very fierce. The Spaniards thought that one of the women in the canoe was a queen, while one of the boys was her son. These Indians were afterward sent to Spain, and were stared at by people who liked to have their blood curdled by the sight of man-eaters.

The early discoverers were so easily deceived by what they saw, and what they fancied they understood in talking by signs with the natives, that we are not sure whether the Caribbeans were so much of cannibals as the Spaniards imagined. They thought that they found parts of a man boiling in a kettle on the island of Guadaloupe; but when we remember that Columbus mistook sea-cows for mermaids, we may be permitted to doubt whether this interrupted meal of the Indians was really a meal of human flesh. It is quite likely, however, that they may sometimes have eaten their enemies in the ferocity of war, as our North American Indians did. All the natives of these islands had the cheerful habit of keeping the bones, or perhaps the heads of their dead friends, about their cabins, and when the Spaniards saw such things among the Caribs, they were likely to think them the signs of cannibalism. The people in Spain, believing all they heard about these fierce captives, thought the "queen's son" had a lion's face, and the crowd looked with shuddering horror at such monsters.

Columbus next sailed near a number of small islands, bare and rugged. There were so many of them that he gave them the convenient name of the Eleven Thousand Virgins. The next land that he discovered was the large island of Porto Rico, which the Spaniards noticed had a very rich soil. The Indians on the ships said that the people who lived here were not Caribs, but that the

Caribs fought with them and carried them off, and that they revenged themselves by eating Caribs on occasion. The same day that the fleet left Porto Rico, land was sighted, which Columbus hoped would prove to be Hispaniola, where he had built the fort of La Navidad.

CHAPTER XXI.

WHAT HAD BECOME OF THE COLONY.

1493.

It was the 22d of November when the fleet reached the end of this large island, which proved to be Hayti or Hispaniola, though Columbus had not seen this part of it before. A boat was sent ashore to bury the sailor who had died of the poisoned arrow of the Caribs. A number of Indians gathered around the white men, wearing gold in their ears or about their necks. Some of these Indians went off to the ships and invited the Spaniards to come ashore, saying that they had plenty of gold. But Columbus did not wish to wait here, so he sent the natives back with some shirts and caps for presents. The fleet presently came to Samana Bay, where there had been a skirmish with the Indians on the first voyage.

Of the Indians Columbus had taken to Spain with him, seven had lived to embark on the return voyage. Five of these died on the voyage out, and there were now but two living, and, indeed, the Spaniards had had a great deal of trouble to keep these two alive. One of the survivors belonged to the party of four young men whom Columbus had carried away from Samana Bay. The Spaniards had made a Christian of this fellow, and, having dressed him finely and loaded him with trinkets, they sent him ashore, hoping he would make Christians of his people and persuade them to become subjects to the Spanish crown. They never heard anything more of him. He probably relapsed speedily into savagery and kept well away from white men.

Columbus made his next stop at a harbor near Monte Christo, thinking that perhaps he would make his settlement here. Some of the men landed to see if this was a good place in which to settle. But the country proved to be low and moist, and the men found two dead bodies here. One of them had a rope of Spanish grass around the neck, and was tied to a stake in the form of a cross. The bodies were very much decayed, so that the men could not tell whether they were Spaniards or Indians, but Columbus began to have fears regarding the fate of his colony. The next day the men found two more bodies farther on, and one of these had a great deal of beard, which made the Spaniards very suspicious that there had been trouble, for the Indians had no beards.

Columbus sailed on to La Navidad, where he had left his colony. It was night when he got there, and as he had been once wrecked on the sand bank here, he now lay off the coast to wait until morning. He caused two guns to be fired, thinking that if the Spaniards were still alive they would answer with a shot from the little fort. There was a dead silence, nor could any fires or other signs of living beings be discovered on the shore. About midnight a canoe slipped stealthily out to the fleet. The Indians on board hailed the first vessel they came to and asked for Columbus. They

WHAT HAD BECOME OF THE COLONY. 123

were shown to the admiral's ship. Columbus was in the cabin, but they would not go aboard till they saw him. When he came out they were still distrustful, until a light was held up so that they could see his face. Then they were willing to climb up on deck. One of these Indians was a cousin of the chief Guacanagari. He brought two masks, decorated with gold, as a present from this chief. The Indians stayed on the ships three hours talking with Columbus. When they were asked about the Spaniards whom Columbus left here they said that some of them had died, that others had been killed in quarrels

THE INDIAN TRUSTS COLUMBUS.

among themselves, and that afterward the country had been attacked by a chief named Caonabo, who lived in the mountains of Cibao, where gold came from. This king had burned the houses of both the white men and the Indians, and that Guacanagari had himself been wounded in the fight, and was lying at a distance from here ill of his wound. They said that this was the reason why he had not come out to the ships, though he meant to come the next day. They also said that some of the Spaniards were alive and had gone away from here, but one of them told the San Salvador Indian, who was interpreter, that the white men were all dead. The men in the fleet would not believe this last story, but took comfort in the hope held out by the other relation.

The next morning every one was looking for a visit from the Indian king Guacanagari. Meantime Columbus sent some men ashore. They found the little palisaded fort of the Spaniards burned and leveled to the ground. A few Indians who lurked about were very shy when the white men tried to come near them. The Spaniards began to be very much afraid that the white men had really been killed by the treachery of Guacanagari. They threw buttons and other trifles to the Indians to encourage them, but they could only coax four men to go aboard the ships with them. These Indians said that the white men were all dead. When they were asked who killed them they answered Caonabo. They went away promising to bring Guacanagari, but the chief did not come. Either he had been concerned in the murder of the whites or he was afraid that he would be blamed for it.

WHAT HAD BECOME OF THE COLONY.

The next day Columbus went ashore and examined the burned fort. He found that the house of the chief, Guacanagari, was also burned. Columbus ordered men to dig up the ground around the fort and to look in the well, for he had told the men whom he left in this fort to bury their gold, or to throw it in the well if they were surprised.

While the men were digging, Columbus marched off to look for a better place to plant his colony. He came to an Indian village, of wretched, damp little hovels, overgrown with grass. The people had fled, hiding whatever they could not take with them in the grass around their houses. In these cabins the white men found things that they thought the Spaniards would not have traded, such as a handsome Moorish mantle, folded just as it came from Spain, stockings, pieces of cloth, and an anchor. They ripped open a basket which had been very carefully sewed up, and saw in it an Indian's head wrapped in a cloth. It was perhaps the head of some ancestor preserved in this way, according to savage custom. When Columbus got back to the ruins of the fort, he learned that the Indians had regained their courage during his absence, and had traded gold worth a mark with the white men who had been left there. They had also showed where the bodies of eleven Spaniards lay. The grass had grown over these bodies, so that the men must have been dead for about two months. No gold had been found buried, and there was an end to the ton of gold which Columbus expected to have sent back to Spain.

The Indians still said that Caonabo had killed the colonists, but they hastened to make complaints that the white men had taken three and four wives each from among the native women, so that it began to be suspected that the dead men had angered the Indians among whom they lived and had been killed by them.

A caravel was sent along the shore to look for a better place to build a town than the disastrous La Navidad. Two Indians came out to talk with the captain of the caravel, whose name was Maldonado, as he was sailing along the coast. One of the Indians was the brother of Guacanagari, and he begged the Spaniards to come and see the chief, for he lay ill of a wound, in his village. So Maldonado went ashore with some men. He found the Indian king lying in his hammock with his leg bound up. He told the same story that the other Indians had about the Spaniards having been killed by Caonabo, saying that he had been wounded in the fight, and showing his bandaged leg. He gave to each of the Spaniards a gold ornament, of a size suited to what he thought to be each man's rank. These ornaments were not very valuable, for the Indians were accustomed to beat the gold very thin in order to make it look showy. Guacanagari begged Maldonado to ask Columbus to come and see him.

Columbus concluded to go. Having eaten an early dinner on shipboard, the admiral and all his principal men went ashore, richly dressed, as became men paying a visit to a monarch. Columbus took some presents with him, and Guacanagari had not forgotten to provide himself with presents in turn. The chief lay in his hammock, and made a polite gesture when the Spaniards entered his cabin. He regretted the death of the white men with tears in his eyes. He told Columbus the same story of their fate, how some had died of disease, others had gone to Cibao and been killed, while the rest were attacked in their fort and massacred by Caonabo. Guacanagari gave Columbus a hundred gold beads, a golden coronet, three small calabashes of gold dust, and eight hundred beads made of stone. Perhaps these beads were like a necklace of chalcedony beads from Porto Rico, which exists to-day. These stones are drilled and polished with wonderful perfection, considering that the natives worked with stone implements. Columbus gave Guacanagari, in turn, some glass beads, hawksbells, knives, pins, needles, small looking-glasses, and copper ornaments, all of which seemed more valuable to the innocent chief than gold.

Columbus had two surgeons with him, and he asked Guacanagari to let them see his wound. One of the surgeons, named Dr. Chanca, said that it would be necessary for the chief to be moved outside, for the cabin was so darkened by the crowd of people that it was hard to see anything. The chief consented, but Dr. Chanca thought that he did this "more from timidity than inclination." The Indian king left the cabin, leaning on the arm of Columbus. When the doctor began to untie his bandage Guacanagari explained that the wound had been made by a *ciba*, which meant a stone. When the leg was uncovered, the doctors examined it, but could find no sign of a wound, though the cunning fellow pretended that it pained him very much. Columbus thought best not to appear to suspect the chief, so he invited him to visit the fleet. Guacanagari went and took supper with Columbus. He was shown everything strange on the ship. He was very much astonished when he saw the horses, for there were no four-footed animals of any size on the island. Columbus told the chief that he would like to build houses here. Guacanagari was willing, but he said that it was a damp place, which was true enough. This Indian king talked a good deal with the finest-looking woman among the Caribbee captives, whom the Spaniards called Catalina.

The next day some Indians came on board the ships, and among them the brother of Guacanagari. It was noticed that he talked with the ten Indian women who had come from the Caribbee Islands, and especially Catalina. When night came, these women dropped over the side of the ship and swam for the shore, which was nearly two miles away. The alarm was given, and the women were chased, but only four were caught, just as they reached shore.

This was too much for Columbus. He thought that the wily Guacanagari had persuaded the women to escape. The Spaniards believed that he wished to add Catalina to the number of his wives. Columbus sent messengers the next morning to demand that the chief should return the Indian women. But the village of Guacanagari was deserted. The inhabitants had decamped in the night in spite of the chief's wound. This was one of the first experiences of white men in dealing with the American Indian, whom they had at first believed to be an innocent creature incapable of guile.

As for the little settlement at La Navidad, many another colony in the New World has had a similar fate, for much the same reasons. The colonists were mostly lawless men, and when they were left where they were afraid of no one, they lived as wickedly as possible, robbed the Indians, whom they thought gentle creatures, of their gold and their women, and, falling out among themselves, killed one another. No doubt also some of them died of fevers, as was always the case in the early settlements in America. It is quite likely that a party of them did march off to Cibao to get gold, and got killed for their pains. It would not have been strange if the Indians among whom they had lived had massacred the others, but all that the Spaniards could afterwards learn seemed to show that the story of Guacanagari was true, in spite of his suspiciously invisible wound and his unceremonious leave-taking with the lovely Catalina.

CHAPTER XXII.

THE INFANT SETTLEMENT AND ITS INDIAN NEIGHBORS.
1493.

The day after the flight of Guacanagari the Spaniards went in boats up the coast in search of a good place to settle. As they rowed along the shore the natives seemed uneasy, and when the white men landed they fled. While the Spaniards were walking around the deserted Indian village, they came upon a savage stretched on the ground, with a gaping wound in his shoulder. On examination, the wound proved to have been made by an Indian dart. The fellow had not been able to run any farther. He said that he had got his wound in the fight with Caonabo. Since Guacanagari had taken himself off with the Indian captives of the Spaniards, the latter had disbelieved his story, but when they found this Indian with a wound real and visible, the story seemed more probable again.

INDIAN IMAGE OF STONE, FROM SANTO DOMINGO.

At last Columbus fixed upon a spot for his settlement, and landed men and animals. The horses had

THE INFANT SETTLEMENT.

been on the ship three months, and were very much in need of pasture and a firm footing. A little city, named Isabella, was laid out with a square and streets. A church, a store-house, and a house for the admiral were begun of stone, a stone wall without mortar was to be laid around the town, while the other houses were made of wood and reeds, like the Indian cabins. Seeds were planted, and every one worked very hard, while Columbus "multiplied himself" to superintend the labor.

Before long the malarial fevers, incident to a new land and a warm climate, smote the little settlement. The settlers were landed in a bad condition to withstand illness, for they had been three months on shipboard, living on salt meat and moldy sea biscuit. It required years of experience to teach colonists to eat the light vegetable food of the Indians, which was more wholesome in a warm climate than their own heavier diet. The Spaniards thought that they could not live without wine and salt meat. They were glad enough just now, however, to get the yams with which the Indians came loaded every day. These people would sell provisions, and even gold, to the colonists for tags off of shoe strings, beads, pins, or pieces of broken dishes.

And now for the first time the white men began to be better acquainted with the Indians. The native men were entirely naked, the women usually wore grass and leaves about their hips, while the more ostentatious had a covering of cotton cloth. For full-dress occasions, men and women painted themselves in various colors, decorating their bodies with crosses and with pictures of animals and cabins, which produced an effect ridiculous enough to the eyes of the new-comers. The Indians also shaved some parts of their heads, and left long tufts of matted hair hanging in other places. "In short," said Dr. Chanca, describing them in a letter, "whatever would be looked upon in our country as characteristic of a madman is here regarded by the highest of the Indians as a mark of distinction."

These people had hatchets and axes made of stone, and very handsomely finished, so that the white men wondered at them. They lived mostly on cassava bread. This was made of the root of the yucca, often called the Spanish bayonet. The root was scraped and strained in a press. The liquor which drained from it was poisonous. The pulp was made into a broad, thin cake, which could be kept a long time. When the Indian wished to eat it he steeped it in water. The savages also ate yams, seasoned with agi-pepper and they had besides what Dr. Chanca described as "a kind of grain like hazel nuts, very good to eat." Of course, this was Indian corn. The meat of the Indians was fish, utias or little rabbits about as big as a rat, together with birds, to which they added "lizards, spiders and worms," according to Dr. Chanca. "To my fancy," said the good doctor, "their bestiality is greater than that of any beast upon the earth." This is the near view of the American Indian, and quite different from the poetical ideas about these people which Columbus had

INDIAN FIGURE IN WOOD, FROM SANTO DOMINGO.

THE INFANT SETTLEMENT.

entertained at first. The lizards with which Dr. Chanca was so much disgusted were iguanas, which sometimes grow to be five feet long. The iguana, which is a sort of lizard with a tail like a lance, can climb trees, notwithstanding its size. It is still thought to be very good eating in the countries where it is found.

Alligators were also classed as lizards by the Spaniards. They found that on a small island near Hispaniola there was what they called a lizard "as big around as a calf," with a tail "as long as a lance."

INDIAN FIGURE OF COTTON, LEATHER, ETC., FROM SANTO DOMINGO.

The men often went out to try to kill it, but were surprised to find that though it was so bulky, it got into the sea quickly enough. This was their first introduction to an alligator, the name of which is derived from the Spanish words "*el lagarto*," that is "the lizard."

The Indians had queer little figures of wood, cotton, or stone in their cabins which they called *zemis*, giving them the names of dead ancestors and holding them in superstitious reverence. When the white men asked the natives what these were, they would say "*turey*," which meant "of heaven," or more properly sacred or mysterious. They also called the strange things belonging to the white men "*turey*." Dr. Chanca once pretended that he was going to throw one of these figures into the fire, upon which the Indians fell to weeping, very much grieved. Sometimes they carried their *zemis* off into the woods and hid them, lest the white men should take possession of them. It was not uncommon, however, for them to steal these prized images of one another. The chief kept his *zemi* in a cabin devoted to the purpose. The Spaniards once entered one of these cabins and found the presiding *zemi* speaking. The white men were skeptical, and, examining the mouth of the deity, they found it contained a small tube, which they traced to a heap of leaves in the corner of the cabin, under which lay an Indian, who was engaged in putting words into the mouth of the idol. The chief begged the white men not to expose his tricks, as he was enabled to govern his people by means of the commands of this convenient *zemi*.

The natives performed some rites in the cabins devoted to the worship of these little figures. In the center of the hut was a carved trencher, on which was placed a fine powder, probably tobacco or snuff. The worshiper put some of this powder with a certain ceremony on the head of the image, and then breathed a portion of it into his own nostrils through two hollow reeds, pronouncing some strange words at the same time.

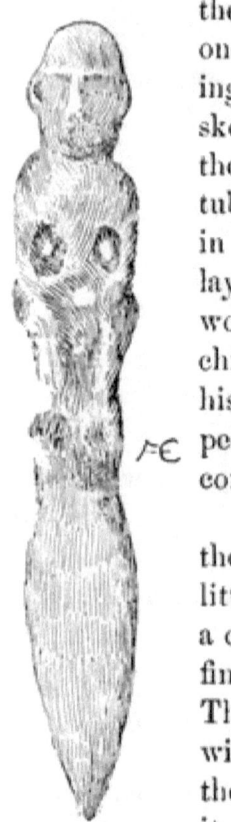

INDIAN IMAGE OF STONE, FROM SANTO DOMINGO.

The Indians had various funeral customs. The body of a chief was often opened and dried before the fire; in other cases the head only was preserved and, again, the body was carried to a cave and left there with a gourd of water and a little bread placed beside it. In other instances the body was burned with the cabin of the dead man. These Indians had a habit of strangling those who were near death, though sometimes they carried them away from their cabins and left them hanging in their hammocks with a little bread and water beside them.

Such relics of these island people as have come down to us—idols, masks, collars, mortars, weapons, and tools—show wonderful workmanship, the highest degree of skill, it is said, that can be attained by men pecking things out of stone with stone implements.

While the Spaniards were noting the customs of the Indians, the latter were making their own shrewd observations with regard to the manners and morals of their new neighbors. "Behold the Christians' god!" they said pointing to bits of gold.

CHAPTER XXIII.

LOOKING FOR GOLD.

1494.

Columbus had chosen the place for the city of Isabella, because he thought that it was nearer to the mountains of Cibao, where the Indians said there was gold. On his departure from Spain he had expected to send back a valuable lading of the precious metal, which was to have been gathered by the settlers at La Navidad. As the men had been massacred, whatever gold they may have collected must have been carried off by the Indians. Columbus wished at least to send back some good news. He was ill himself of the same fever that troubled so many of his men, but he resolved to send Alonzo de Ojeda, with fifteen men, to the place the Indians had told about, to see if there was any gold there. The Spaniards had heard so much about the dreadful Caonabo, or "lord of the golden house," as his name meant, that they were afraid of him, and Ojeda was no doubt chosen on account of his courage. This Ojeda had once amused Queen Isabella in the following fashion: The queen was in a great church tower in Seville, called the Giralda. High up in the air a beam extended out from the tower. From this beam the people below looked like ants. Ojeda walked briskly out on the beam, quite as though he were walking about his own chamber. When he got to the end of it, he stood on one foot for a moment and then, turning about, walked back again. He next stood on the beam, braced one foot against the wall of the tower and threw an orange to the top of it. This feat had attracted a good deal of attention, but Ojeda was really doing a braver thing when he ventured into the country of a chief who had slain the first company of Spaniards that had gone there to look for gold.

Ojeda and his men had to cross many rivers before they reached the mountains. They followed an Indian trail and climbed up into the mountain country. No Caonabo appeared to stop the way, and the Indians were friendly. They washed grains of gold out of the sands of the brooks and gave them freely to the white men. There was certainly gold here. Ojeda and his men picked up some nuggets, one of which weighed nine ounces. They were sure that there must be a great deal of ore in the mountains, for the Indians dug no deeper than the length of a hand

THE GIRALDA TOWER, SEVILLE.

in looking for it. Ojeda and his men went back with their specimens of gold. The next day, another young gentleman, named Gorvalan, who had been to another place where the Indians said there was gold, returned with specimens of the metal. There was great excitement in the settlement. Columbus wrote a very hopeful letter to send back to Spain. Dr. Chanca also wrote in his letter that "the king and queen might now consider themselves the most wealthy sovereigns in the world," for, said he, "on the return of the ships from their next voyage they will be able to take back such a quantity of gold as will fill with amazement all who hear of it." So twelve ships sailed back to Spain, laden only with the news of gold mines, of laurel trees whose bark smelled like cinnamon, of trees bearing beeswax or producing wool and cotton, and other marvels such as men can always see in a beautiful new land before they have had time to put their new discoveries to the test.

One of the things that Columbus wrote in the letter that he sent back in these ships was a proposal that the Spaniards should capture the natives of the Caribbee Islands and send them to Spain as slaves, exchanging them for cattle, which the people at Hispaniola would need very much. He argued that this would be an advantage to the savage slaves, since they would become Christians in this way and learn not to eat their fellow-men. As the Portuguese made slaves of the negroes of Africa, it is not strange that Columbus should have thought of making slaves of the Indians. Indeed, the poorer classes in Europe were held at this time in a sort of bondage, and there was no sentiment in favor of human liberty. The great discoverer at this time planted the seeds of slavery in these beautiful islands. In the hands of cruel and greedy adventurers, this slavery was soon to sweep away the whole Indian population.

While Columbus was still ill of malarial fever a plot was formed against him among some of the men of Isabella. Already the colonists had begun to be homesick. They found that there were no sudden fortunes to be picked up in the New World, while there was a great deal of hard work, for which they had not bargained. A man named Cedo, who was an assayer of metals, gave it out as his opinion that there was no gold on the island, or at least so little that it was not worth looking for. When the Indians brought large grains of gold, he said that they had been melted and had been a long time gathering, having been handed down from generation to generation among the natives. The malcontents made a plot, under the lead of an officer named Bernal Diaz, to seize the ships in the harbor and sail to Spain. But Columbus, hearing of the scheme, put the leader in prison and punished some of the others.

The admiral, having now pretty well recovered from his illness, got ready to make a journey in person to Cibao. For fear of any more mutinies, he had all the arms and ammunition in the town stored in one of the vessels in the harbor. He then gave his brother Diego command of Isabella while he should be gone. Columbus wanted to make quite a display and overawe the Indians this time, so he took four hundred men with him, and he caused them all to be dressed in the most brilliant colors and march to the sound of drums and trumpets, with banners flying, followed by a train of Indians from around Isabella.

The little army set out on the 12th of March, 1494, and marched for the first day through a plain and across two rivers. At night they camped at the foot of a rocky pass, through the Monte Christo Mountain range, which Columbus named El Puerto de los Hidalgos, or the Pass of the Gentlemen, because some cavaliers had gone ahead and opened the road for the others to pass through. The next day men, horses, and mules climbed up the pass. When they reached the summit they looked down upon many leagues of beautiful plain beyond, crossed here and there by the silver thread of a stream, columns of smoke rising from Indian cabins, graceful palms and other noble tropical trees growing everywhere, while the whole charming stretch of level land was bordered by the hazy lines of distant mountains. This grand valley, which is famous to-day for its noble beauty, was named by Columbus the Vega Real, or Royal Plain.

The Spaniards descended the slope and began to march through the Vega Real. Columbus ordered the horsemen to go first because the Indians were very much awestricken at the sight of horse and rider. In fact, they thought that horse and man were all one animal, and were quite astonished when they saw the animal walking around in two divisions, as it seemed to them when the men dismounted. The savages had, in fact, no good opinion of horses. Such large animals, they felt certain, would eat them.

There were many Indian villages in the Vega. The little round cabins were built of reeds with thatched roofs, and doors so low that the inmates had to go on all fours in entering them. As the brilliant army neared an Indian village, horsemen in advance, banners flying and trumpets and drums sounding, the simple natives fled or crept in at the doorways of their cabins, barring them with a few reeds. The Indians who had come with the Spaniards from Isabella walked into a native house and helped themselves to anything they might find in it, without any ceremony. The owner never showed any displeasure, but when the Indians tried this practice among the whites, they were soon made to understand that it was not a Christian custom.

The army presently arrived at a river which Columbus named the River of Reeds. The Spaniards encamped for the night on the beautiful banks of this stream. Before sleeping they bathed in its waters. In the morning they crossed in canoes or on rafts, and swam their horses over. The next day they marched through magnificent forests, where they saw many strange fruits which they tried to imagine the same as fruits they had known in Spain. Columbus named the next stream that he crossed the River of Gold, because some particles of gold were found in its sands. The third river that lay in his course ran across translucent pebbles, which gave it a green look, so Columbus called it Green River. All of these streams were the Yaqui or its tributaries. The following day the army reached the foot of some steep mountains, that the discoverer called the Gates of Cibao. The next day the march was through a rough and rugged country. Often riders had to descend from their horses and scramble up steep places, leading their animals. From this point Columbus sent back some mules to Isabella to bring more provisions, for the journey had been longer than he had expected, and the Spaniards thought that they could not eat the Indian food. The following day found the little army in the country of Cibao, which was very different

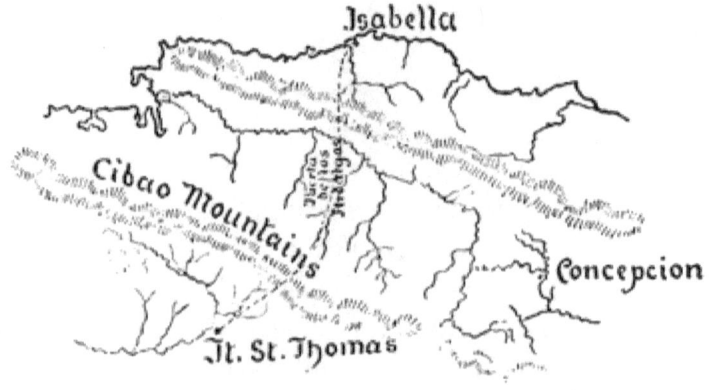

MAP OF THE ROUTE FROM ISABELLA TO CIBAO.

from the Royal Plain. This was a land of rocks, covered only with such plants as could grow in a stony soil, with a few pine and palm trees here and there, while little streams carrying particles of gold in their sands ran down from the mountains. The Indians met the Spaniards with presents of provisions and grains of gold which they had gathered in the streams for them.

Columbus made up his mind to build a fort in this country, so that the Spaniards would have a place in which to store their gold and to take refuge in, in case of an attack. He named his proposed fort St. Thomas, as a sort of pious jest, because the discontented ones at Isabella had doubted the existence of gold here unless they might see it and touch it. When the men were digging for the foundations of this fort they came across what seemed to them a sort of nest of straw, in which were, in place of eggs, several round stones as large as oranges which seemed to have been worked by the hand of man. The Spaniards wondered at these, and thought they looked as though they were meant for cannon balls, for stone cannon balls were used in Europe at that time. It is likely that they were really stone heads for Indian war clubs, which had been hidden here or perhaps buried with some Indian as his cherished treasures. Such round stones were also used sometimes to crush the grains of Indian corn.

CHAPTER XXIV.

TROUBLES OF THE COLONY.

1494.

Columbus left a captain named Pedro Margarite and fifty-six men to build Fort St. Thomas, and began the journey back to Isabella. At Green River he met his mules returning with provisions. They had lost some time at the River of Gold, because it was swollen by rains and there had been trouble about crossing it. When Columbus reached the River of Gold, he had to stop there some time himself to wait for the water to fall. The people brought him food, and sold it to him for trifles. Columbus and some of the wiser Spaniards began to eat the food of the country in order to set a good example to the others.

It was the 29th of March when the admiral got back to Isabella. He was much pleased to find that melons which had been planted less than two months before, were now ripe. In twenty days cucumbers had grown large enough to eat, while a wild vine which had been trimmed was loaded with grapes, green peas were ready for picking, and some wheat had ripened. Every seed that was put into the rich soil sprang up, fruit stones germinated, and sugar-canes grew, so that Columbus found every reason to be delighted with the fertility of the beautiful island.

TROUBLES OF THE COLONY.

The colony was not so prosperous, however, as its fields and gardens. The moist, warm climate which made things grow so fast was not suited to Europeans. There was a great deal of sickness, and there had been many deaths. The young Spanish gentlemen of noble families who had come over expecting to get suddenly rich, or at least to have some fine adventures, were disgusted when Columbus made them do their share of work with the commoner sort of people in the building of the town. They remembered that the admiral was a foreigner, and only a peasant by birth, and they hated him. When men grew sick there was no one to nurse them, and they died of fever and homesickness. Columbus, as the head of the colony, was likely to be blamed for the misfortunes which befell these young gentlemen. The gloomy end of so many men of good families was long remembered in Hispaniola. Years after this, when Isabella had been abandoned, because it was unhealthy, there was a story that two Spaniards once wandered into the deserted town. In one of its grass-grown streets they saw two rows of hidalgos, or Spanish gentlemen, in old-fashioned dress. The two Spaniards were astonished to see strangers in this lonely place, and asked them who they were and where they came from. The gentlemen did not answer, but politely raised their hands to their heads to take off their hats by way of salute. Horrible to relate, their heads came off with their hats, and the headless gentlemen presently had the good taste to vanish. The beholders, according to the story, almost fell dead with fright, and after this the tale of the dead gentlemen who were so polite as to doff their heads became the stock ghost story of the island. It serves to show how long and vividly the misfortunes of these early settlers were remembered in Hispaniola.

Columbus had hardly reached Isabella on his return when he had news from Fort St. Thomas that all the Indians had fled from the country, and that Caonabo was coming to burn the fort. The admiral was not greatly alarmed by this news. He was meditating a voyage of discovery, for he had not given up his notion that he was on one of the islands at the eastern extreme of Asia, and that by going westward he must reach a civilized country. He began to make ready for the voyage. Provisions were running low at Isabella. The biscuits were almost gone, and the flour was used up. There was some wheat, but there were no mills to grind it in. The colonists were starving in a bountiful land. In order to give them something to do, so that they might not be brewing mischief, and hoping to get them used to eating the food of the country, Columbus made all the able-bodied men in Isabella, except a few workmen whom he wanted to build mills and some sailors for the ships, into a little army, and sent them to march through the island and overawe the Indians. He sent this body of men as far as Cibao under the charge of Ojeda. When this captain reached Fort St. Thomas he was to take command of this fort, and let Pedro Margarite take the lead of the little army.

Ojeda had got no farther than the River of Gold before he got into trouble with the Indians. Three Spaniards going from Cibao to Isabella had been granted by a chief three Indians to carry their baggage over the river. When the three Indian porters had got half-way across the river, they turned and ran away with the bundles of the Spaniards. The native king, instead of punishing his thievish subjects, took possession of the bundles himself, in all simplicity. The Spaniards demanded their property in vain. Ojeda, appearing on the scene, cut off the ears of one of the thieves and sent nearly the whole royal family in irons to Isabella. Columbus thought best to make an example of these fellows, to save the Spaniards from further trouble. A chief, who lived near the unlucky one whom Columbus was about to punish, came to Isabella in a great hurry, to beg for mercy for his friend. This chief had been very kind to the white men, but Columbus, nevertheless, had his prisoners taken to the public square to have their heads cut off. The friendly chief begged with many tears for the lives of the captives, and Columbus finally forgave them.

Having settled the affairs of the colony as well as he could, Columbus set sail on the 24th of April, in his three smaller vessels, to look for Asia.

CHAPTER XXV.

THE VOYAGE OF DISCOVERY.
1494.

The admiral, having heard that Guacanagari had come back to his old home, stopped at the harbor of La Navidad to see him. The chief, however, took a hasty leave when he saw the ships appear. So Columbus sailed on for Cuba. He thought that Cuba was part of the main-land of Asia, and he wanted to know more about it and especially to claim it for Spain before the Portuguese should reach it by the opposite route. He soon approached the eastern end, which is now called Point Maysi. From this place the admiral set out to sail along the southern shore of Cuba. After coasting for some distance he anchored in a harbor which is now called Guantanamo. The entrance to this harbor was narrow, but within it seemed like a lake surrounded by mountains and bordered by blossoming trees. Columbus could see two cabins built of reeds, and the smoke of fires on the beach. He landed with some armed men and the San Salvador Indian, who went along as interpreter, but the wigwams were empty and the fires had been deserted. Apparently the Spaniards had broken up a feast. There were fish, utias or little rabbits, and guanas or big lizards, hanging on the trees or roasting over the fires. As the Spaniards had been living meagerly of late, they sat down to eat without more ado, though they left the guanas untouched, for they considered them a kind of serpent, and felt much disgust at the thought of eating them. After they had feasted, the men, strolling about in the woods, happened on seventy Indians huddled together upon the top of a high rock. When the Spaniards tried to get near them they fled, with the exception of one very bold man, who stood ready to run at the first sign of danger. The Indian interpreter was sent out to talk with this brave.

MAP OF THE VOYAGE ALONG THE COAST OF CUBA.

The interpreter having satisfied the natives that their strange-looking visitors meant them no harm, they presently came forth from their hiding-places. Their chief, they said, had sent them to the sea-shore to get fish for a feast which he was going to give to another chief, and they were cooking the provisions as the only means of keeping them from spoiling in a warm climate. The savages gave themselves no trouble because the strangers had eaten their food. They said that one night's fishing would make that good. Columbus, however, paid them in beads and hawkbells, so that white men and Indians parted very good friends, after a hearty hand-shaking all around.

As the ships sailed along the coast crowds of Indians—men, women, and children—looked at them from the land. They held up fruits and provisions to tempt the strange voyagers ashore, and sometimes they paddled out in their canoes, bringing cassava bread, fish, and calabashes of fresh water as offerings to the heavenly beings. The admiral never failed to send the simple creatures away happy with gifts of trifles. He dropped anchor again in another noble harbor. Here there were Indian villages and cultivated spots of ground which looked in the distance like orchards and gardens. We must remember that Columbus and his men were always straining their eyes to see some sign of the civilization of eastern Asia. The people of this bay were as friendly as possible. The admiral asked them where gold was to be found. They directed him to a large island south of them. Columbus was tempted to go out of his course to look for this island. He steered directly south. Presently the lovely shores of Jamaica came in view. He thought this the most delightful land he had yet seen.

It is strange to see how variously the Indians were affected by the first sight of white men. In some places they fled, in others they came out to meet their visitors with perfect confidence, while in still other places they were disposed to fight. The Indians of Jamaica met the ships in a fleet of large canoes, giving the war-whoop, and threatening the Spaniards with their wooden lances. Columbus, as usual, avoided a battle. He wished to make friends with them and learn something from them about the world in which they lived. Looking for a harbor where he could get fresh water and careen one of his ships to calk her, he found a bay where the savages were very fierce. They were decked with black war-paint and gayly colored feathers, and they threw their spears at the white men and yelled in true Indian style. As it was necessary to get rid of these furious fellows before the ship could be hauled ashore and careened, Columbus sent some cross-bow men in the boats to attack them. Spanish arrows fired from cross-bows soon threw the warriors into confusion. The men then landed, let fly another volley, and set a fierce dog on the Indians. This is the first time that we hear of a dog being used in Indian warfare; it was, in fact, a custom brought from Europe, where the use of these animals in war was not unknown. Large dogs were new to the natives, who had only small dogs that could not bark.

Columbus named the island Santiago, but it has retained its more beautiful Indian name of Jamaica. The Indians, after they had been cured of their first fury, were friendly enough, bringing the Spaniards plenty of fresh provisions. These people had very large "dugout" canoes, made of immense mahogany trees. These were carved and painted at the bow and stern. It is said that one of these canoes was ninety-six feet long and eight feet wide. Columbus did not stay long at Jamaica. Probably he did not find the prospect of gold sufficient to tempt him to give up his search for India along the coast of Cuba. Just as he was about leaving Jamaica an adventurous young Indian came out to the ships and begged to go with the white men. His family followed him, imploring him not to go, but he persisted. He sailed away with the Spaniards, and we do not know what became of him.

Columbus crossed again to Cuba, steering for a cape which he named Cabo de la Cruz, or Cape of the Cross, and the cape is still called by this name. He landed at a large native town. The chief of this place told him that when the Spaniards sailed along the northern shore of Cuba, on the first voyage of Columbus, the Indians who had seen the white men told the news from one to another, and that it had reached him. The admiral asked these savages whether Cuba was an island or a continent. They answered that it was an island, but so large that no one had ever seen the end of it. This answer left Columbus as uncertain as ever. He sailed on west, and presently found himself in a very large bay or gulf. A severe thunder-storm struck him here. This tempest put the ships in a good deal of danger while it lasted, because there were many sand-banks and keys or little rocky islands in this bay. The farther the ships sailed, the more of these islands there were. The sailor at the mast-head could see them as far as his eyesight reached. Some were small and bare, others were green, while still others were covered with forest trees. It was a very beautiful sight, and Columbus called this the Queen's Garden. The Queen's Garden was, however, a very dangerous place for ships, and the admiral hardly dared to sleep night or day, for fear of another accident like that which had happened on his first voyage. He might have stood farther out to sea and avoided these keys, but he remembered that Marco Polo had described the coast of Asia as having a great many islands near it, and he expected soon to reach some rich country. It was a most anxious time for Columbus, for often the ships had to be towed out of a dangerous place, while sometimes they actually touched upon sand-banks in spite of all his care.

While the admiral was sailing among these islands he came upon some Indian fishermen, who were too much absorbed in their pursuit to be frightened at the sight of the strange vessels. They motioned for the whites to keep still and not disturb their fishing. So the Spaniards watched them a while. The Indians tied a line to the tail of a small fish which had hooked fins upon its back. The story goes that these fish very obligingly went and hooked themselves into the bodies of large fish; but it seems more likely that the large fish swallowed the little fish, and so got caught themselves. The Spaniards invited the fishermen on board. The Indians gave the whites their fish, and would have given them their fishing-tackle and the gourds in which they carried their drinking-water, but Columbus would not take these. He made the fishermen happy by some cheap presents.

The ships sailed on, the men still admiring the little islands, on some of which they saw brilliant flamingoes, while on others were tortoises. They observed that these creatures laid their eggs in the sand and left them there to be hatched by the heat of the sun.

After the hot tropical day in these regions the clouds gathered at sunset every evening and there was a terrible thunder-shower, which cleared away when the moon rose. The nightly tempests gave Columbus a great deal of anxiety in these dangerous shallows.

CHAPTER XXVI.

ALONG THE COAST OF CUBA.
1494.

For a little time Columbus found it clear sailing, having got out of the Queen's Garden at last. He stopped at a large Indian village for food and water. The natives brought the white men some kind of a bird to eat, which they took for a dove. Finding that these birds had a peculiar taste, Columbus had the crop of one of them opened, and thought that it contained sweet spices. As spices were wished for next to gold, the admiral believed this a good sign. He tried at this place, as usual, to find out what the Indians knew of the geography of the land that they lived in. The old chief of the village said that farther on there were a great many more islands, and that the sea was shallow. The Indians had never heard, they said, that Cuba had any end to the west—at least, they were certain that one could not reach the end in forty moons. They said that there was a country west of here called Mangon, where one might learn more about it.

Mangon, Columbus thought, sounded like Mangi, which was the name of the southern part of China, according to Marco Polo. He asked the Indians more about it, and got from them some story about the people who lived there having tails and wearing clothes to hide them. In truth, Columbus had got into a region of romance once more, for he had reached a land where his interpreter could not understand the language of the natives, and so conversation was carried on by signs. Now, Columbus remembered that Sir John Mandeville, the Englishman who had traveled in Asia after Marco Polo, had said that some of the naked tribes of Asia believed that the people who wore clothes did so to conceal tails, as they could think of no other reason for wearing clothes.

Ever hopeful, and expecting soon to reach a country where people went clothed, Columbus presently came to a sea rendered milky in color by fine white sand mixed with the water. The ships were soon entangled among many little islands again, but Columbus pushed ahead, believing himself on the eve of making some notable discovery. He stopped in a great bay, and sent some men ashore for water. The forests were so high and thick that it was impossible to tell whether there were any people living here or not. While the men were filling the water barrels, one Spaniard scrambled about in the woods with his cross-bow, looking for game. He came running back to his companions and said that he had seen some thirty Indians, among whom were three white men, one of whom was dressed in a long white robe, while two wore tunics down to their knees. He said that he had shouted for his companions, for he was afraid to meet so many alone, and with that the whole troop had fled. The sailors all took refuge in the ships immediately, for there seemed to be something terrifying to them in the idea of meeting men in clothes. As for Columbus, he was pleased to hear the story, for he thought that he was now about to find a civilized country, or that at least there was a civilized land in the interior.

The next day the admiral sent an armed party of men on shore, telling them to go forty miles inland, if need be, to find these men who wore clothing. They traveled through the forest until they came to a plain overgrown with tall and matted grass, in which they became so tangled that they presently returned. But Columbus did not give it up, and sent another party out the next day. These men had not gone far before they found the track of some large animal. It was no doubt the foot-prints of an alligator, but they took it for the tracks of nothing less than a lion or a griffin, and made a hasty retreat for the ships. They had found on their trip great cranes feeding in natural meadows, had smelled spicy odors, and had seen immense grape-vines climbing up the trees. Columbus afterward sent some clusters of grapes from this part of Cuba to Ferdinand and Isabella, as well as some of the water of the milky sea.

The admiral sailed on until he came to some Indian cabins. The natives were naked, but Columbus was not dismayed by this, as he imagined that they were only fishing tribes, and that more civilized people lived inland. These Indians brought out provisions to the ships. Columbus tried to learn something from one of them about the country, but as he had to talk by signs, he got a queer story as usual. This time it was a tale of a chief living in the mountains, who wore a long white robe and spoke only by signs. Beyond this place the admiral found only a lonely coast where no human beings were to be seen. Still, he did not for a moment doubt that he was near the civilized parts of Asia. He made a plan for exploration which was worthy of his great mind. He would continue on past India to the Red Sea and so cross over to Joppa on the Mediterranean, and sail back to Spain, or, better still, sail clear around Africa and beat the Portuguese on their own ground. In this way Columbus thought to be the first man to go around the world. This was a noble plan, and perhaps Columbus would have tried to carry it out if he could. He would then have found that Cuba was only an island, and would have discovered the main-land of America lying in his way, if he had sailed on to the west; and in reaching Mexico he might have found something like the civilization that he was looking for, as well as gold enough to fulfill the hopes of Spain. But his ships were very leaky, his stock of sea-biscuit was scanty and spoiled by being wet, and his men, incapable of his great conceptions, were clamorous to return to Hispaniola.

Columbus sailed westward until the 13th of June, and still found no end to Cuba. The sailors agreed with him that this was no doubt the main-land of Asia. But before he turned back, the admiral sent a notary around the three ships to take the oath of every man that Cuba was the continent of Asia. This seems a strange thing to do, but Columbus began to find out that his men could tell different tales about his discoveries under different circumstances. Everybody, down to the ships' boys, took their oath, and it was then proclaimed that if an officer contradicted this statement he was to pay a fine of ten thousand maravedis, while a common sailor would get a hundred lashes and have his tongue cut out.

While this strange Old World proceeding was going on to prove that Cuba was a continent, it is said that a ship's boy at the mast-head might have looked over the islands and seen the Gulf of Mexico beyond. But Columbus turned back, and as he steered southeast he discovered the large Island of Pines.

CHAPTER XXVII.

THE RETURN TO HISPANIOLA.

1494.

Columbus stopped at the Island of Pines for wood and water. He tried to sail around the south side of this island to get away from the little keys, but he got into a deep lagoon instead of a channel, and had to go back. The men were much discontented at having to sail back ever so little. Having got out of the lagoon, Columbus went around the north of the island, where the ships sailed through a milky sea and an inky sea. Again they must worm their way through dangerous passages between little islands. Once the admiral's ship ran aground. It was impossible to pull her off the bar, and she had to be towed over, which strained her badly and made her more leaky than ever.

The little vessels at last reached open water. Sweet odors came from the shores. On the lonely coast where they had been the men had to live on a pound of moldy sea-biscuit and a small measure of wine a day. They were glad enough now to anchor in the mouth of a river and feast on utias, birds, cassava bread, and tropical fruits brought to them by the Indians. Columbus had a wooden cross put up here, as he did in many other places, by way of taking possession. After the cross had been put up mass was said. The old chief of the country "assisted very decently" at the mass by making various motions. When the ceremony was over he gave the Spaniards to understand that he comprehended perfectly that they were thanking God, and that he knew that the souls of the good would go to heaven, while the body would return to the earth. He said that he had visited Jamaica and Hispaniola and knew the principal people on these islands, and that he had traveled to the east of Cuba, where there was a chief who wore a robe like the Spanish priests. As this Indian king said all this by signs, we may be permitted to doubt whether he said anything of the sort, and believe that what he really said was something quite different. When Cuba came to be better known, no people were found in it who wore clothes, so that the tales of people who wore robes grew no doubt out of the strong belief of the white men that they were in Asia.

From this river Columbus struck out more to sea, to avoid the shallows of the shore. On the 6th of July there set in a terrible rain which seemed like another deluge. What with leaking from below and with rain from above, the ships were pretty nearly submerged. The poor sailors toiled at the pumps without any apparent effect. Columbus and his men suffered very much, for they had to support all the work and anxiety of the voyage on spoiled and scanty food. When they got fresh provisions from the natives they could not keep them over one night, so warm was the climate. Columbus, worn out by his trials, vowed that he would never subject himself to such vexations again.

After eleven weary days the ships made land at

Cape Cruz. The Indians brought them cassava bread, fish, fruits, and other things to eat, and the hungry men were comforted for a time. Necessity had made them begin to like the native food. The wind was contrary for sailing to Hispaniola, and so Columbus struck over to Jamaica and coasted the southern shore of this island. Perhaps he had not yet given up his notion that there was gold on this island. He beat to the east for nearly a month along the shore of Jamaica, the winds being very unfavorable. The enthusiastic explorer was delighted with this his last discovery. The natives were now very friendly, and came to the ships in canoes with provisions. At one place three canoes paddled out to meet the ships. In one of these, which was carved and painted, was a chief with his wife and two daughters. This chief moved in state. His attendants wore head-dresses of gay feathers, while round his own head were strings of colored stones, with a large piece of gold in front. He wore two plates of gold hanging from his ears, a string of white beads hung around his neck, while he was adorned with a belt of colored stones about his waist. His wife was decorated with bead ornaments, and wore also a small cotton apron, and some cotton bands about the arms and legs. The eldest daughter had a girdle of stones, but the other one was probably too young for finery, for she wore nothing whatever. It is said that this chief wished to go away with the Spaniards, but Columbus would not take him, knowing how much Indians suffered when they attempted to live in a state of civilization.

It was the 20th of August when Columbus sighted

the western end of Hispaniola. He was not sure what island it was, until a chief came off to the ships who called Columbus by name and used words which he had learned of the colonists. The homesick sailors were delighted. They were yet, however, a long way from Isabella. Columbus lost sight of two of his ships at one time, and sent some sailors to climb to the top of a small rocky island to look for them. The men did not discover the lost ships, but they killed six sea-wolves and a number of birds. These creatures were so unused to men that they could be knocked over with sticks. After six days of waiting the lost vessels rejoined the admiral. The little fleet then sailed westward along the southern shore of the island in view of a beautiful plain, where there were many inhabitants. Some of the people came out to the ships and told Columbus that men from Isabella had visited them. He asked them how things went with the colony, and they said "Well." Columbus was much relieved when he heard this, for he was anxious about the settlement. He sent nine men overland to Isabella to carry the news that he was coming.

By the middle of September Columbus was still coasting Hispaniola, when he was struck by a very bad storm. He took refuge behind a small island which lay near Hispaniola, but he was very anxious about his other ships, which were in the open sea. They rode out the storm in safety, however, and joined the admiral when it was over. The discoverer had planned to extend his voyage to some of the Caribbee islands, but he had been so anxious and slept so little for so long a time, that he fell ill of a fever at this point, and lay as

THE RETURN TO HISPANIOLA.

though he were dumb, blind, and senseless for many days. His men hastened to Isabella with him.

The first person that the sick discoverer saw when he came to consciousness was his brother Bartholomew, whom he had not seen for more than eight years. Columbus must have been delighted to encounter this brother once more, as he seems to have been very fond of him. Bartholomew Columbus had come back to Spain when he had heard of the great deeds of Christopher. The king and queen had received him very kindly, and had given him the command of some ships which were going out with provisions for the colony.

VIEW OF THE SOUTHERN COAST OF HISPANIOLA.

CHAPTER XXVIII.

WHAT HAPPENED IN THE COLONY IN THE ABSENCE OF COLUMBUS.

1494.

The sight of his brother was the only pleasant thing which happened to the sick discoverer when he reached his colony. Everything had been going as badly as possible. Pedro Margarite, who had been left by Columbus in command of a small army, instead of exploring the island in accordance with the orders of the admiral, encamped in the Vega Real, among the Indians. Here the Spaniards acted much as the first colonists on the island had done: they devoured the food of the natives, eating more, it was said, in a day than would supply a native for a month. They robbed the Indians of their wives and led wicked, lawless lives in every way. In vain Diego Columbus had remonstrated with Margarite. Margarite thought himself above an upstart family like that of Columbus. Many of the colonists, belonging to great Spanish families, having been angered that Columbus had forced them to work, took the part of Margarite. Father Boil, who was the head of the priests in the colony, was among the malcontents. Margarite and Boil did not think it best to wait for Columbus to return, but took themselves off in the ships which had been brought over by Bartholomew Colum-

WHAT HAPPENED IN THE COLONY.

bus. They wished to hurry back to Spain in order to tell their tale first to the king and queen.

Meantime, the soldiers, left to themselves, wandered about the island robbing and oppressing the Indians at their will. The natives presently began to take revenge in true Indian fashion, falling suddenly upon any small bands of white men that they might find and massacring them. One chief put to death the Spaniards who had quartered themselves in his town. After this he set fire to a house where there were forty sick men.

The fierce chief Caonabo thought it a good time to attack Fort St. Thomas. But this fort was in the hands of Alonzo de Ojeda, and he was quite another sort of a man to deal with. He had fought the Moors and been engaged in private feuds and duels many times, having never yet lost a drop of blood. He always carried with him a small painting of the Virgin, which he believed protected him from harm. When he was out on an expedition, he would take this picture from his knapsack whenever there was a chance, and, hanging it against a tree, say his prayers to it. Like John Smith, the warrior of Jamestown, and Miles Standish, the Indian fighter of Plymouth, Ojeda was a little man, but very bold and strong.

Caonabo found Ojeda ready for him. The fort was well built, and surrounded by a river on three sides and a ditch on the other. Not finding the white men off their guard, as they had hoped, there remained nothing for the natives to do but to starve them out. They besieged the fort, but Ojeda gave them plenty to do, falling upon them at any favorable moment, and slaughtering them right and left at the point of the sword. Indians are never good at a siege. They began to fall away one by one, until Caonabo was forced to go himself for want of an army. But the chief did not give up his hope of exterminating the white men. He prowled around Isabella, and saw how weak it was and how many of the people were ill. There were five great chiefs in the island, and Caonabo made a plan to get them all to join him, in order to get rid of the Spaniards once for all. The five chiefs were easily persuaded, except our old friend Guacanagari, who once more took the part of the white men. As he was the chief whose people lived nearest to Isabella, he was an important ally.

After Columbus had returned from his voyage, he was sick for some time. He made Bartholomew his lieutenant or *adelantado*, for this brother was a man of a great deal more force than Diego. While Columbus was still lying ill Guacanagari came to visit him. He told Columbus how he had remained friendly to the white men in spite of the persuasions of the other chiefs. He said that this had made the other chiefs angry with him, and they had killed one of his wives and stolen another. He wanted Columbus to help him punish his enemies. When he talked about the massacre of the first colony it was with tears in his eyes, so that Columbus began to think as much of Guacanagari as he had at first.

At present the Indians were menacing a small Spanish fort called Magdalena, which was near the great Vega. Columbus sent some soldiers to relieve this fort. He also sent for the principal chief of this region, whose name was Guarionex. He explained to Guarionex that he had only sent out these soldiers to relieve his fort and punish the chief who had massacred so many Spaniards while he was away. He also said that the bad actions of the Spaniards while he was away had been done in disobedience to his orders. In order to get this chief to feel friendly toward the settlement, he persuaded him to allow his daughter to marry his Indian interpreter, who was a San Salvador Indian. In this way Columbus coaxed away another chief from Caonabo. He did not know how to deal with Caonabo himself, however, for it was impossible to hunt him out of his mountains, and there was no knowing when he might fall upon the settlements. At this moment the bold little Captain Ojeda offered to go with only ten men to capture the dreaded chief and bring him alive to Isabella. Columbus gladly accepted this offer, though it was doubtful what would be the outcome of such an adventure.

CHAPTER XXIX.

OJEDA'S ADVENTURE AND THE WAR THAT FOLLOWED.
1494-1495.

OJEDA chose ten men to go with him, and, after arming and mounting them well, set off on his hair-brained adventure. He traveled many miles through the forests before he reached the home of the mountain chief. Probably his picture of the Virgin went with him and hung on more than one tree by the way. Caonabo was not alarmed when these eleven white men entered his town, for they were too few to do him any harm. Ojeda pretended to have come on a friendly errand from Columbus, to bring the chief a valuable present. The bold Spanish soldier soon made himself a prime favorite among the Indians. He could do all kinds of feats, to their great admiration, and they already knew him to be a great warrior.

Ojeda took a strange way to coax Caonabo to go to

OLD CANNON FROM THE FORTRESS OF SANTO DOMINGO.

Ojeda praying to his picture of the Virgin.

the settlement. It seems that the Indians were very much charmed with the chapel bell at Isabella. One can fancy that an Indian, who delighted in the tinkle of hawkbells tied on his arms and legs when he danced, would be much pleased with the sound of a large bell. The Indians thought that the chapel bell was certainly *turey*, or supernatural. When they saw the Spaniards hurry to church at the sound of its ringing they imagined that the bell talked to them. Ojeda now offered to give Caonabo this wonderful bell if he would go to Isabella with him. Caonabo thought he would, but he took care to take his warriors along. Ojeda objected that this did not look like a friendly visit, but Caonabo said that it would not do for a person of his importance to go visiting with fewer attendants. This was a very good excuse, but Ojeda did not like the looks of this manœuvre. He knew that Columbus wanted to avoid war and either make peace with this chief or capture him. He pretended to be satisfied, however, and traveled on with the Indians. When they were near the river Yaqui Ojeda one day showed Caonabo a set of burnished steel manacles. He told the chief that these beautiful ornaments came from the *turey* of Biscay, Biscay being the Spanish town where iron was manufactured. He also said that these ornaments were worn by the kings of Spain at their most solemn dances.

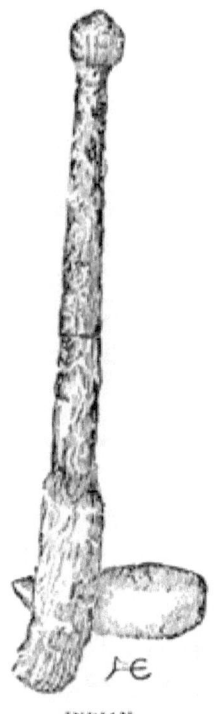

INDIAN BATTLE-AXE.

The flattered chief consented to put them on, after having bathed in the river. The next step was to persuade Caonabo that it would be a fine thing to ride into Isabella on horseback wearing these royal ornaments. The chief consented to mount behind Ojeda, dressed in manacles. He no doubt felt that he cut a fine figure in the eyes of his wondering subjects, decked with shining ornaments and daring to ride one of the dreaded horses. Ojeda and his men dashed around among the Indians, making wider and wider circles, until they got out of sight in the forest. The soldiers then drew up around Caonabo, brandishing their swords and telling the chief that they would kill him if he made a sound or tried to get away. They hastily tied him with cords to Ojeda, and they all rode away for Isabella, leaving the Indians far behind. They had a long and dangerous journey before them. They thought best to avoid Indian villages or gallop through them at full speed, and they suffered greatly from hunger and watchfulness.

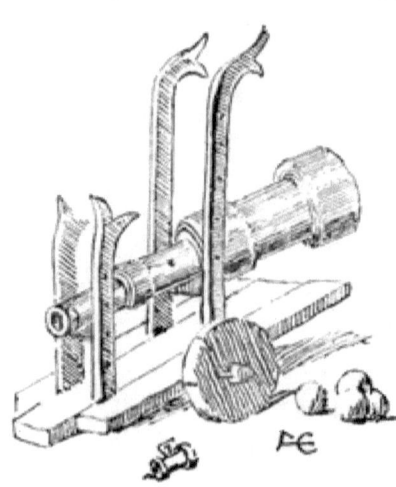

CANNON OF COLUMBUS'S TIME.

Fancy the surprise in Isabella when the brave little Captain Ojeda entered the town with the dreadful Caonaba tied behind him. The chief bore his misfortunes stolidly, in Indian fashion. For want of a better place, Columbus kept him a prisoner in his own house, which was small. The captive chief, in chains, could be seen by passers-by through the open door. When Columbus, who kept up a good deal of dignity as viceroy, entered the house, all who were there rose in his presence. The Indian chief, however, declined to rise, but he always got up when the small Captain Ojeda entered. The Spaniards asked Caonabo the reason of this. Columbus, they told him, was *guamiquina*, or chief over all, and Ojeda was only one of his men. Caonabo answered that Columbus had not dared to come to his house and make him a prisoner, while Ojeda had.

By capturing Caonabo Columbus did not get rid of Indian wars. One of this chief's brothers presently marched forth to attack Ojeda, who was at St. Thomas again. The little captain, however, rode out to meet the Indians, and soon put them to flight, killing many of them and capturing the chief's brother.

As was always the case with later colonies in the New World, the men were generally half starved, though living in a plentiful land. The supplies furnished by the Indians were uncertain, as they were a very indolent people and did not feel obliged to raise more food than was necessary for their own immediate wants. The colonists, so long as they had to work for the colony in general, never succeeded in planting enough to support themselves. The famine in the colony of Columbus was only ended by the arrival of four ships from Spain loaded with provisions. The admiral sent back by these ships five hundred Indians to be sold as slaves in Spain. This was a cruel measure, into which Columbus was probably pushed by the demand upon him to make the colony immediately profitable, while it was argued that the poor natives were thus put where they might stand a chance of being converted to Christianity. The wars with the Indians had perhaps also excited a hatred of the race. Columbus sent over what gold had been gathered, but this was probably not a very large amount, considering that the settlers had spent more time in squabbling and idleness than in gold-digging. The Indians were sold in Seville, but they died speedily in their new and hard life.

During all this time Columbus was ill. It was not until five months after he had first been taken sick on shipboard that he recovered his usual health. Indian war was constantly threatening the settlement, and by April, 1495, it broke out. All of the chiefs, excepting Guacanagari, banded together to attack the white men, another brother of Caonabo taking his place as chief of the tribe. They were on the warpath now, making their way toward Isabella.

STONE-CARVING, FROM SANTO DOMINGO.

Columbus made haste to muster his army. It was very small—only two hundred footmen and twenty horsemen—but there were also twenty bloodhounds. The white men wore steel armor, and carried cross-bows, swords, lances, and the awkward gun called the arquebuse. Guacanagari and his warriors followed the Spanish force, but they were of no use to the white men. The little army marched up over the Pass of the Hidalgoes and down into the beautiful Vega Real. The Indians sent scouts ahead to see how many there were of the white men. The savages were not able to count above ten, so they carried ears of corn with them and shelled off a grain for every man they saw in the army of Columbus. As they brought back a very small amount of corn to represent the Spanish army, the Indian chiefs felt sure of success.

Columbus divided his army into several parts, each of which attacked the Indians from different points. The sound of drums, trumpets, and fire-arms drowned the war-whoops of the natives. The horses trampled them under foot, their riders dealt blows to right and left

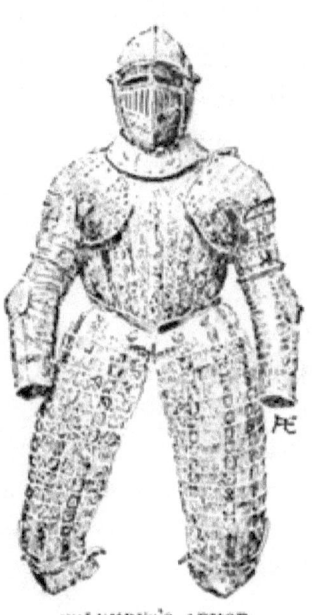

COLUMBUS'S ARMOR.

with their swords, the bloodhounds chased down their prey and tore the helpless creatures to pieces, while the arquebuse did its share in the deadly work. The warriors fled in every direction, or begged for mercy from the tops of rocks and precipices. Many were killed, and many more were taken prisoners.

After the battle Columbus made a tour through the known part of the island and reduced it to subjection. The Indians were forced to pay tribute. Each savage over the age of fourteen was made to pay a hawkbell full of gold-dust. In the places where there was no gold, cotton was taken in its stead. A much larger tribute was exacted of the chiefs. The brother of Caonabo had to give half a calabash of gold. When the Indians had paid their tribute they were given medals of lead or leather to wear around their necks, and any Indian found without his medal was punished. This tribute was a terrible burden to the Indians, to whom work made life unendurable. It bore also very hard upon the chiefs, who were leaders among the Indians rather than kings, as the Spaniards thought, and could not, it is probable, exact much tribute from their so-called subjects, and so were little richer than other Indians. It was found to be so hard for the natives to furnish so much gold that the tribute was reduced to half a hawkbell of gold-dust, a hawkbell full being worth about five dollars. Meantime, there was such complete peace that a white man might go from one end to the other of the island unarmed and meet with no harm.

CHAPTER XXX.

TROUBLE FOR COLUMBUS, AND A NEW GOLD MINE.
1495-1496.

Columbus had no sooner settled the affairs of the island than his enemies in Spain made him fresh trouble, and they could not be dealt with so easily as the simple Indians. The two runaways, Margarite and Father Boil, had made as bad a story as possible of the troubles of the colony, blaming Columbus for everything. As it was very hard for the king and queen to know the real state of the case at so great a distance, they sent a man named Juan Aguado out to the colony to inquire into the state of affairs there. This Aguado had been one of the officers of Columbus on his second voyage out. In his letters to court, Columbus had recommended him and Margarite to the royal favor. Now, however, we find that they were both his enemies.

When Aguado landed at Isabella Columbus was in the interior of the island. Aguado took no notice of Bartholomew Columbus, who was governing in his brother's absence. He caused the letter of credence given to him by the king and queen to be proclaimed by sound of trumpet It read:

"Knights, esquires, and other persons who by our orders are in the Indies, we send to you Juan Aguado, our groom of the chambers, who will speak to you on our part. We recommend you to give him faith and credit."

Of course, everybody who was discontented complained to Aguado, and there were many such people, while Aguado made the most of his little time of authority. Meantime, Columbus hastened to Isabella. People expected that there would be some sort of an explosion when Aguado and the proud discoverer met. But there was nothing of the sort. Columbus received Aguado courteously, caused the letter of credence to be proclaimed again by trumpet, and said that he was ready to obey the sovereigns in everything.

After Aguado had meddled in the government of the island and had spent some time hearing the complaints of discontented white men and Indians, this gentleman got ready to leave. Columbus also thought best to go back to Spain and try to undo what his enemies had been doing against him at court. When the ships were all ready to set sail one of those terrible hurricanes which occur sometimes in tropical countries struck Hispaniola. A wind from the east and a wind from the west seemed to meet and engage in a terrific war to the sound of thunder. The whirlwind tore over the country, pulling up great trees by the roots, and loosening rocks in the mountains, which crashed into the valleys below. The lighter houses were blown away, and people fled for safety. The ships in the harbor were whirled about, their cables broken, and they were either sunk or wrecked on the shore, while the men on board of them were drowned. After three hours the storm was over. The Indians called this kind of storm *furicanes* or *uricanes*, and that is how they have come to have the name of hurricane. The four ships which Aguado had brought over were wrecked, as well as two others that were in the harbor. There was only the Nina left, and she was badly damaged. Columbus and Aguado did not care to sail to Spain in the same vessel, so that there was nothing to do but to wait until another could be built out of the timbers of the wrecked ships.

While the vessel was being built something interesting happened. There was a young Spaniard named Miguel Diaz, who had had a fight with another man and wounded him so badly that it was thought that he would die. Afraid of being punished as a murderer,

Map of Hispaniola

young Diaz ran away with several other men who had been in the fight with him. They wandered about the island until they came to an Indian village in the southern part of Hispaniola, which stood where the city of

Santo Domingo now is. The Indians were friendly, and the white men lived among them. There was a female chief in this village—one Catalina. Young Diaz became her husband after the Indian fashion, and they lived together for some time.

After a while Diaz began to be weary of the society of Indians. The Indian queen soon discovered what made him sad. Afraid of losing her husband, Catalina thought of a plan which would bring the Spaniards to live in her town, so that Diaz would not lack for company. She accordingly told him that there was a fine gold mine near by, and that this would be a much better place for the Spaniards to build a town than Isabella, which was unhealthy. The young man found what Catalina had told him to be true; so, taking the Indian guides, he set off for Isabella, hoping that the news of a gold mine would buy him forgiveness for his crime. He went into Isabella secretly at first, but found that the man whom he supposed he had killed had got well again. He was not afraid now to go boldly to Columbus with his piece of news. Columbus wanted to move his settlement to a healthier spot, and would also like to have some good news to take to Spain, so he sent his brother Bartholomew with a party back with Miguel Diaz to see if his tale were true. Bartholomew Columbus crossed the island, and found a richer gold field than had yet been discovered. In some places he saw pits dug, as though the Indians had in some former time had the industry to mine a little.

The admiral was much pleased when Bartholomew brought back such good news. He ordered a fort to be built at these mines, so that they might be worked.

Catalina tells Diaz of a new gold-mine.

Miguel Diaz now became quite an important person. Catalina got her reward, for Diaz did not desert the wife who had brought him such a good dowry.

The very lively imagination of Columbus sometimes carried him far, and made him think of many things not so reasonable as his notion of finding land by sailing to the west. He still thought himself to be in the far East, and he now fancied that the gold diggings just discovered were the ancient mines of Ophir, from which Solomon got his gold for building the temple at Jerusalem. Many people in a later period have had similar fancies, and Ophir has been placed successively in California and Australia by fanciful writers.

CHAPTER XXXI.

IN SPAIN.

1496.

Columbus sailed for Spain in March, 1496, with some two hundred and twenty-five sickly or discontented men, who wished to return home, and thirty Indians, among whom were Caonabo, one of his brothers, and a nephew. The admiral promised this chief that he would take him to Spain and then return him to his home. It was not known then that by steering somewhat north the trade winds could be avoided, so Columbus, who steered directly east, had a very tedious voyage. The clumsy ships of that time could make little head against the wind, and the two little vessels beat about for nearly a month without getting out of the West Indies. Columbus anchored at length at the island of Guadaloupe to make cassava bread, for he was afraid that his provisions would not hold out for the voyage.

When the Spaniards tried to land, fierce Indian women opposed them, armed with bows and arrows. Columbus thought that this must be the island in Asia which Marco Polo had told about where Amazons lived. Some of the Spaniards busied themselves making bread, while others made a trip inland and returned with some captive women and children. One of these women was a chief's wife. She had nearly strangled the man who had tried to catch her, and he was only saved by the other white men coming up in time. These women were naked and wore their hair long. They tied cotton bands very tightly around their legs and ankles to make the calves of their legs look plump, as large calves were thought a trait of beauty with them. As Columbus considered that Guadaloupe was the gate, so to speak, to many other islands, it seemed best to him to send back the Indian women, in order that the people might not fear the white men, so they were all sent ashore, except the ferocious chief's wife and her daughter, who chose to stay among the Hispaniola Indians on shipboard.

Having laid in a store of twenty days' bread, besides what he already had, Columbus set sail. The ships labored against contrary winds, and after a month's sailing had not yet neared the Old World. The provisions were almost gone. Each man was allowed but six ounces of bread a day and a little bottle of water. Time wore on, and starvation became imminent. Some were in favor of devouring the Indians, after the example of the detested Caribs, while others were for throwing them overboard, so that they need no longer be fed out of the scanty stock. But Columbus would hear nothing of the sort. He and his pilots had some dispute as to where they were. Some thought that they were in the English Channel and others that they were off France, but Columbus thought that they were near the Azores. Land was presently seen which Columbus said was Cape St. Vincent near Lisbon. He ordered sail to be taken in for the night, at which the hungry men grumbled. They would rather be cast headlong on the coast of Europe than stay another night famishing on the water. The next day found them at the very land that Columbus had said. During the long voyage the chief Caonabo had died. He was the first of many native American chiefs who tried to make a confederacy to oppose the oncoming tide of European emigration.

When the discontented colonists disembarked in Spain, lean with famine and sallow from the malarial fevers of the New World, it was said by people who saw them that all the gold they had brought back was in their faces. Columbus was beginning to be something of a devotee under the troubles which had come upon him. Though he was First Admiral of the Indies, he went ashore unshaven and dressed in the gray robe and cord of a Franciscan monk.

We know that Columbus had held extravagant ideas about the countries he went to discover. He had to swallow his disappointments and make the most of naked barbarians, spices whose existence was only suspected, and gold which was yet undug. But the people in Spain who had not seen, as the great admiral had, the wonderful beauty of these tropical islands, began to imagine his discoveries of small account. The tales of the runaway captain and priest and of the disappointed colonists who had returned sallow and thin made them think that the Indies must be a poor world after all.

Though Ferdinand and Isabella may have had doubts as to whether Columbus was a good governor from the tales they had heard, they still did not forget that he was really a great man and had done them a great service. As soon as they knew that he was in

Spain they sent him a kind letter, asking him to come to court. Columbus accordingly traveled toward the city, where he was to meet the king and queen. He knew that people had begun to say that there were no riches in the West Indies, so he made a display, as he journeyed, of head-ornaments, armlets, anklets, and collars of gold, as well as Indian masks and queer images of wood and cotton. The Indians that he brought with him were decorated with gold trinkets and dressed after their savage fashion. When Columbus passed through a large town he put a heavy gold chain and collar on the neck of the brother of Caonabo, who figured as king of the golden province of Cibao.

Columbus was very well received at court. He showed the curiosities he had brought with him, gave an account of his trip along the extreme coast of Asia, which was really Cuba, and asked for eight ships with which to make further discoveries in the New World. The ships were promised, but it was a long while before the money for such an undertaking could be procured, for Ferdinand was an ambitious king and had many enterprises in Europe which he thought more important than the exploration of far-away lands. One of the king's cares at this time was the sending of a great Spanish fleet to Flanders to bring back the Princess Margarita, who was to be married to Prince Juan, the Spanish heir. The sons of Columbus, Diego and Ferdinand, who had now both become pages to Prince Juan, were present at this ceremony when it took place.

During this time of waiting and neglect for Columbus others were allowed to go out on voyages of discovery. This was a much cheaper way for the rulers of Spain to push forward discovery, and they began to disregard their agreements with Columbus. "Now," said Columbus bitterly, "there is not a man down to the very tailors who does not beg to be allowed to become a discoverer."

Provisions were sent out to the colonies, but Columbus waited long for his ships. Meantime Isabella remained kind to him. She granted him again all the rights that he had asked for when he went on his first voyage, and also made them hereditary, for Columbus wanted to found a great family. The crown prince did not live very long after his marriage. Though the queen was almost heartbroken at the loss of her only son, she remembered the two sons of Columbus who had been in the service of the dead prince, and made them pages to herself.

After two years of waiting, a squadron of six ships was granted to Columbus. It was now so hard to get people to go to the New World, on acount of the bad reports that had been made about it, that criminals were permitted to go from the prisons instead of taking their punishment at home. This was a bad method of settling a new land, for where such people went there was sure to be trouble.

Just as Columbus was about to set sail on this new voyage, the fiery temper which is supposed to go with auburn hair like his got the better of him, and in a dispute with a man named Ximeno, he knocked him down. Columbus afterward regretted bitterly this fit of anger, and it is said to have done him more harm with the king and queen than all the complaints from Hispaniola.

CHAPTER XXXII.

COLUMBUS SETS SAIL ON HIS THIRD VOYAGE.
1498.

It was the 30th of May, 1498, that Columbus set sail on his third voyage to America. He took a course much farther south than he had done before. One reason of this was that he wished to avoid a French squadron, which might make him trouble. Another reason was that he had an idea that the main-land of Asia lay farther to the south than he had sailed before. He had also still another notion in steering southward. A lapidary, or a man skilled in the knowledge of precious metals and stones, had told him that the most precious articles came from the hottest regions of the earth. He was of the opinion that if Columbus would get nearer the equator, and find blacker races of men, he would also discover more valuable articles.

At the Canary Islands the admiral divided his fleet, and sent three ships directly to Hispaniola, so that the colonists need not want for food. He sailed himself first to the Cape de Verde Islands, which were barren, and looked very different from the beautiful tropical islands of America. From the Cape de Verde Islands he steered southwest until he was near the equinoctial line. He now found himself becalmed in a region of terrible heat. The seams in the ships gaped, the tar melted, the salt meat began to spoil, and the hoops shrank from the barrels of wine and water. The holds of the ships were so hot that the men could not stay down there long enough to attend to the meat and the leaky barrels. For eight days the heat lasted. Columbus said that he thought the men would have died had the sun shone, but it was cloudy and rained most of the time. He gave up steering any farther south, and when the east wind sprang up he sailed to the west. With the east wind the weather became more endurable.

The ships sailed directly west for seventeen days. The heat was getting very severe once more, and the supply of water was almost exhausted. Columbus therefore changed his course to the northwest, hoping to strike the Caribbee Islands. On the 31st of July there was but one barrel of water left, when a sailor, who climbed to the maintopmast, saw the peaks of three mountains rising above the horizon. The men sang their hymn of thanksgiving, and Columbus named the land Trinidad, or Trinity, on account of its three peaks. He steered for a cape which had a rock lying off it, that looked like a galley under sail. Columbus named it Cape Galea, or Galley, and it is now called Cape Galeota. The island was very beautiful, and as "fresh and green as the gardens of Valencia in March," said Columbus. He had to sail some distance along the southern coast of Trinidad before he could find good bottom to anchor in. He only stopped long enough to take in a barrel of water, and then sailed to a sandy point at the western end of Trinidad, where he anchored once more.

He now ordered the casks to be repaired, wood and

water to be taken in, and gave the people a chance to rest from their voyage. They found many tracks on the shore which they thought were made by goats, but probably they were the tracks of deer. The day after the ships had anchored a large canoe put in an appearance, with twenty-four Indians in it. They were young men with graceful figures, and lighter complexions than any Columbus had seen before. They wore cotton scarfs, woven out of various colors, bound around their heads, or about their hips in place of breeches. They were armed with bows, arrows, and shields made of wood. They called to the white men from their canoe, but they kept at a safe distance, and if they thought that they were drifting dangerously near they paddled off again. Columbus caused basins of polished metal and looking-glasses to be held up so that they might see them, hoping that these shining articles would tempt them to come on board. After a long while they moved a little nearer, but they were very wary. The admiral wished very much to speak to these Indians, so he ordered a drum to be played on the quarter-deck, and told some of the young men on board to dance, thinking that the Indians would come up to see the fun. The latter, however, so soon as the dancing began dropped their paddles, strung their bows, and let fly at the dancers. The music and dancing ceased very suddenly, and Columbus ordered that the compliment should be returned by cross-bow men. When the Spanish arrows began to fly the Indians took refuge under the poop of one of the smaller ships. The captain of this ship talked with the Indians as well as he could. He gave their chief a coat and hat, and agreed to meet them on the shore. While he went to the admiral's ship to get permission to do this the Indians went away.

Columbus found that there was a strait between Trinidad and another land which lay west of it, and which he called Gracia. He did not know that Gracia was the mainland for which he had looked so long. The currents rushed through this strait with such fury that it was like row after row of breakers, and Columbus feared that the ships would be carried upon hidden rocks if they attempted this channel.

The admiral was suffering from gout, and his eyes were inflamed, but he dared not sleep when he was on unknown coasts. In the middle of the night, while he was on deck, he heard a dreadful roaring sound, which came from the south and grew nearer and nearer. Presently he saw that a great wave, as high as a ship, was coming toward him, making a frightful noise as it came. The discoverer was seized with terror lest his vessels should founder when the wave struck them. But the ships rose to the giant swell and it passed on, roaring for a long time in the strait between Trinidad and the mainland of South

COLUMBUS SAILS ON HIS THIRD VOYAGE.

America. This strait seemed so terrible to Columbus that he named it the Mouth of the Serpent. The immense wave which he had seen was produced by the waters of the great river Orinoco flowing into the sea and through the strait into the Gulf of Paria.

The next day the admiral caused the Mouth of the Serpent to be sounded, and found that the waters were sufficiently deep, though there were contrary currents. He sailed through the strait safely, and came to still water on the other side. Columbus was now in the great Gulf of Paria, but he still thought he was in the open sea and that he had passed between two islands. The men were surprised when they drew up some of the water to find it quite fresh. This freshness was caused by the inflowing waters of the Orinoco, which, besides running out at its principal mouth, also sends streams through a delta into the Gulf of Paria.

A TRINIDAD PALM.

CHAPTER XXXIII.

COLUMBUS DISCOVERS PEARLS.
1498.

Columbus now sailed northward until he came to two high headlands. The one on the east was part of the island of Trinidad, while that on the west was the end of a long peninsula which belonged to the mainland of South America, though Columbus did not yet know this. Between these headlands was another narrow strait where the water roared in a fearful manner. The admiral thought this still more terrible than the Mouth of the Serpent, so he called it the Mouth of the Dragon. He turned and sailed along the coast of Paria westward, thinking that Paria was an island and that he could find some other way into the sea than through the dreadful Dragon's Mouth. As he sailed he found that the water grew more and more fresh. He presently saw a spot where he thought that the land looked as though it were cultivated. Columbus wanted very much to talk with some of the natives, so he sent the boats ashore. There were signs of men here—fires, footprints, the leavings of cooked fish, and a house without a roof—but no people were seen. The shore was hilly and there were fruit trees and a great many monkeys.

Columbus proceeded, hoping to find level land, where

there would be more likely to be many people. He anchored at length in the mouth of a river. A canoe with several Indians in it paddled up to the nearest ship. The captain of this ship pretended that he wanted to go ashore with the Indians and jumped into the canoe, upsetting it. He and his men then caught the Indians in the water and took them to Columbus, who gave them beads, bells, and sugar—treasures which made them forget the way in which they had been entrapped. They were then sent ashore, and it was not long before the ships were surrounded with canoes, in which were Indians quite willing to accept gifts of bells, beads, and sugar also. They told Columbus that their country was called Paria, and that farther west there were more people. So Columbus took four of these Indians with him and sailed on. He came to a beautiful coast, very thickly peopled. The Indians came out to the ships in great numbers. They wore cotton scarfs so beautifully colored that they looked like silk. These they wound about their heads and loins. These people had also plates and collars hung around their necks made of a mixed metal which contained some gold, and which they called *guanin*. Some of them had strings of pearls about their arms, a delightful sight to Columbus. They told him that they got these pearls on the northern shore of Paria and showed him the shells of pearl oysters.

Columbus wanted to get some of the pearls to show to Ferdinand and Isabella, so he sent the boats ashore. The Spanish sailors who went ashore in the boats were received very kindly by the natives. Two chiefs, whom the Spaniards took to be father and son, followed closely by a throng of Indians, advanced to meet the strangers. They took the white men to a very large house, built with sides and not round and tent-like as the island houses were. This was probably a council house. The men stayed in one end of the building and the women in the other. The Indians brought bread, fruits, and a sort of wine for the strangers to feast on. There was nothing to do but to make signs of friendship, for the white men and Indians could not understand one another. The Spaniards were next taken to the house of the younger chief, where they were made to eat again. These Indians were tall and lithe, with long, smooth hair. Their heads were bound with embroidered handkerchiefs, and men and women tied long cotton scarfs about their middle. They all wore some kind of ornaments on their breasts and arms. Some wore pieces of the inferior gold hanging low on their bosoms; others had strings of pearls on their arms. The Spaniards bought some of the pearls in exchange for hawksbells, which to an Indian had this advantage over pearls, that they would tinkle, as well as look bright. These Indians had handsome, light canoes, with cabins in the middle of them. Columbus called this place "The Gardens" because it seemed so pleasant to him.

The great discoverer was almost blind now from the malady that afflicted his eyes, so that he could scarcely see the lands which he found. The provisions were spoiling, and it became necessary to make all haste for Hispaniola. He thought that Paria was an island and that he would soon reach the end of it by sailing to the west, and thus be able to pass out toward the north.

He could see parts of the main-land, in the bottom of the gulf, and he thought that these were also islands. He sent one of his light caravels ahead of him to try to find the passage. The vessel presently returned with the report that there was only a large gulf with four smaller gulfs opening into it. Columbus was disappointed that he could find no opening outward to the north, south, east, or west except the two roaring months. Finding that the water was so fresh in this great gulf, he concluded that there must be some large river running into the ocean here, and the reason that these two channels were so boisterous was that the great body of fresh water and the sea were having a struggle, the river water trying to run out while the ocean tried to run in. This was a right conclusion, and yet Columbus was at first not nearly so sure that he had found the main-land as he had been when he coasted Cuba.

There was nothing to do but to try the dreadful Dragon's Mouth, which Columbus did. While he was sailing through the rough channel he tasted the water and found that on one side of the channel it was sweet, while on the other it was salt, showing that the ocean and the river water were running in and out. Columbus named the Gulf of Paria the Gulf of Pearls, because he had found the Indians wearing pearls here, and he thought that the pearls had been found in this gulf. In those days people had a belief that the pearl oyster made pearls out of drops of dew which fell from trees into the water. As there were oysters here clinging to the roots of the trees which grew over the water and heavy tropical dews, there must be pearls; nothing seemed more simple. In fact, however, the Indians got all their pearls, as they said, on the northern side of Paria—not in the gulf, but in the ocean.

After Columbus left the gulf he sailed to the west along the northern coast of Paria, to make sure whether it was an island or not. He presently discovered the islands of Margarita and Cubagua, which afterward became the seats of great pearl fisheries. When the ships were sailing near the small bare islands of Cubagua the admiral came upon a number of Indians who were pearl fishing. They fled when they saw the white men. A boat was sent after them, and the men noticed that one of the Indian women had a great many strings of pearls around her neck. The Spaniards broke up a plate of Valencia ware, which was a kind of bright-colored porcelain, and exchanged these pieces of crockery for some of the woman's pearls. Columbus afterward sent some men ashore with smashed crockery and hawksbells, which they traded for pearls.

The admiral sailed straight from the pearl fishery to Hispaniola. He wished to strike this island near the new city of Santo Domingo, which had been founded in his absence. But the current which starts from the Mouth of the Dragon, and is now called the Gulf Stream, carried him to a point on the island about fifty leagues west of Santo Domingo. Columbus sent ashore to get an Indian messenger to carry a letter to his brother Bartholomew, to let him know that he was coming. Six Indians came out to the ships, and one of them carried a Spanish cross-bow. Columbus did not like the looks of this. He sent his message, however, and then sailed on for the settlement. His brother

Bartholomew sailed out and met him before he got there.

Columbus had some very fanciful theories about the discoveries he had made when he found the land of Paria. He suggested that the earth was pear-shaped and imagined that somewhere in the interior of this land lay the Garden of Eden upon a great eminence which formed the top of the pear, from which flowed the quantities of sweet water he had found in the Gulf of Paria. Writers on Columbus have held him almost insane for this notion. They do not seem to have known that this theory was founded on the authority of Sir John Mandeville, the English traveler, who followed Marco Polo into the unknown parts of Asia. Sir John Mandeville in his book of travels describes the earthly paradise as placed on a part of the world so high that it almost touched the circle of the moon, inclosed with a wall covered with moss, in the center of which was a fountain that cast out four great rivers, up which no man could sail because the waters of the streams ran in such great waves and roared so that it was impossible to row or sail against them. The mind of Columbus was full of legends of the East, and it was not strange that the tumultuous passes and the great flow of fresh water into the Gulf of Paria suggested to his mind the roaring floods of Sir John Mandeville's paradise.

CHAPTER XXXIV.

WHAT HAPPENED IN THE COLONY WHILE COLUMBUS WAS AWAY.

1496-1497.

TOWER AND FORTRESS OF SANTO DOMINGO.

When Christopher Columbus had sailed away to Spain in 1496 from Hispaniola, Bartholomew Columbus crossed the island to build a fort at the place where the Indian wife of Miguel Diaz had shown her husband gold. He called this fort St. Cristoval, but the workmen who built it dubbed it the Golden Tower, because they found grains of gold when they were digging for it.

Don Bartholomew, as he was called, had trouble to furnish his men with food. The Indians were not provident people, and they could not be depended upon to willingly provide much more food than they wanted themselves. For this reason Bartholomew Columbus had soon to leave his fort with only ten men to guard it and a dog to hunt utias or little rabbits for them, so that they need not starve. He marched away with his other men to the Vega Real, where he collected the tribute, which was much of it paid in food. No doubt the Indians thought it very hard that these greedy armed men should sit down among them and make them pay tribute, a thing before unknown to them in their simple way of living.

There came ships from Spain in July, 1496, with provisions and a letter to Don Bartholomew from his brother Christopher, telling him to send to Spain as slaves all Indians who had had anything to do with the killing of white men, and to found a town at the mouth of the Ozema River, which was near the gold mines that Miguel Diaz had discovered. Accordingly, three hundred Indians were shipped off to Spain to be sold for slaves, and Bartholomew journeyed across the island again to build a town near the new fort of St. Cristoval, so that ships could land there. This new town, Santo Domingo, afterward became the capital of Hispaniola, and finally gave its name to the island. It was in a beautiful spot, and it was near here that Miguel Diaz lived with his Indian wife, who received the white men as kindly as she had promised to do.

After Don Bartholomew had built a fort, which was to be the beginning of the new city, he went to make a visit to a chief called Behechio, who had not yet made the acquaintance of white men. The country of this chief was called Xaragua, and was the whole west end of the island. He had a sister named Anacaona, which is said to mean flower of gold. She had been the wife of Caonabo, but had returned to her country when this chief had been made a prisoner. She is said to have been a handsome Indian. Don Bartholomew marched through the native towns in the most showy

THE GUANA.

style to the music of drum and trumpet, with the cavalry in advance and banners flying.

Behechio met the little Spanish army with a large force of armed warriors. The Indians, however, laid down their bows and arrows, and merely asked what the Spaniards had come after. Don Bartholomew answered that he had only come for a visit. So the chief, who had been suspicious at first, dismissed his warriors, and sent messengers ahead to his town to order a feast for his guests. When the white men neared the town of Behechio, thirty Indian women came dancing out to meet them, waving palm branches. The married women wore aprons of embroidered cotton, but the young women were entirely naked, with only a cotton fillet around their heads. After these women came Anacaona, who was carried on a sort of litter by six Indians. She wore only an apron, but she had wreaths of red and white flowers about her head, neck, and arms.

The Spanish officers were feasted at the cabin of Behechio. The meal consisted of utias, river and sea fish, roots, fruits, and the guana. As this last was a large lizard, the Spaniards could never be persuaded to eat it, calling it a serpent. Anacaona now pressed Don Bartholomew to taste the loathsome dish. He did so out of politeness, and the old story says he found the flesh so delicate to his tongue that he fell to without fear, seeing which his men were not behind him in greediness. The Spaniards were lodged at night in the cabins of the Indians and slept in their cotton hammocks. The natives entertained their visitors for two days with games. One of these represented a battle. The Indians were so earnest in their entertainment that four men are said to have been killed in the sport, at which the Spaniards begged the natives to leave off.

Don Bartholomew presently came to business and told Behechio that he had come to his country to arrange for a tribute to be paid to the Spanish sovereigns. Of course, there was nothing for the Indian chief to do but to make the best of it, since these white men with their terrible arms and horses were quartered in his midst. He was not pleased, however, for he knew that the Indians had suffered very much in other parts of the island by being forced to gather gold for the Spaniards. He told Bartholomew that he was aware that gold was what the white men most wanted, but that there was no gold in his country, and his people scarcely knew what it was. Don Bartholomew answered that he would take cotton and cassava bread instead of gold, at which the chief looked much relieved.

Meantime at Isabella there was the old story of illness and idleness, of men who would not raise their own food and depended for support on the supplies from Spain or upon the Indians. These Indians, who lived near Isabella, getting tired of feeding the white men and playing the slave generally, had fled to the mountains. Of course there were all sorts of grumbling and discontent at Isabella. To give the men something to do, Don Bartholomew began the building of two caravels at that place. He sent the sick men inland, where they would get better air and food. He also had a chain of forts or

FORTRESS AND SHORE OF SANTO DOMINGO.

strong houses built between Isabella and Santo Domingo.

Two faithful priests had been living for some time among the Indians on the Vega Real, trying to make

CHURCH OF SAN ANTONIO, NEAR SANTO DOMINGO.

Christians of them. The total number of converts was sixteen, all of one family. The priests spent a great deal of time trying also to convert the chief of the Vega, Guarionex, and they taught him and his whole family the Pater Noster, the Ave Maria, and the Creed, all of which this Indian family repeated daily, probably regarding them as some superior kind of incantations. The chief, however, suddenly relapsed from Christianity when some Spaniards carried off his favorite wife. The priests were discouraged, and got ready to move to some other Indian country, but before they went away they fixed up a small chapel with an altar, crucifix, and images in it for their convert and his family of fifteen persons.

No sooner were the priests gone than some Indians went into the chapel, broke the images, and buried them in a field near by. Complaint was made to Don Bartholomew, and he, very unwisely, took the affair in hand. It was the days of the Spanish Inquisition, and pious people were great bigots. The crime of the image breakers was thought to be of the very worst sort, and so they were burned to death as a punishment. It ought to be said that Don Bartholomew also punished the man who had seduced the chief's wife.

The Indians were very angry, and they planned to rise suddenly and massacre the white men. The handful of men in one of the posts called Fort Concepcion heard of this plot. Don Bartholomew was at Santo Domingo, and they wished to send him word so that he might save them from being exterminated by the savages. They did not dare send a letter openly by an Indian messenger, for as he had no clothing in which to hide it, the letter would be taken away from him, the Indians having learned by this time that among white men paper could talk. The men at Fort Concepcion rolled a letter up and put it into a hollow reed or cane, telling the messenger to use the reed for a staff. The Indian proved a cunning fellow. When he was stopped by hostile Indians he pretended to be dumb and lame. He made signs to show that he was going home, and limped along painfully, leaning on his staff. When he got well out of sight, however, he left off limping and took to his legs in a very lively way.

As soon as he received the letter Don Bartholomew hurried to the rescue with a body of men. It was none too soon. The warriors had got together from a great distance, and were ready to strike the blow. Bartholomew Columbus seems to have been a very good Indian fighter. He divided his men into different parties, and fell on the native villages secretly at night, when the warriors were all asleep. The plan was to carry the chiefs off prisoners, and thus leave the Indians without leaders, Don Bartholomew undertaking to capture Guarionex himself. The Spaniards accomplished the feat, and took fourteen chiefs captive without bloodshed. The natives surrounded Fort Concepcion, where their leaders were imprisoned, and howled dismally. Bartholomew caused the two chiefs whom he thought most to blame to be put to death. He forgave Guarionex and the others, and released them. In truth, the white men did not think best to be too severe with the Indians. They began to be afraid they would flee to the mountains, when there would be no tribute of gold, yams, potatoes, Indian corn, or cassava bread.

Don Bartholomew now got word from Behechio that his tribute was ready, so he marched off to the country of Xaragua. The Spaniards were received in the same friendly way that they had been before. There was a cabin full of cotton waiting for the white men, and Behechio offered them all the cassava bread they wanted. Bartholomew Columbus was very glad to accept this offer, as the Spaniards were in their usual state of want. He sent to Isabella for one of the new caravels that had been building to come around and carry away the bread and cotton. Meantime he waited in

Xaragua, where he was very well treated and feasted on Indian dainties.

The vessel came, after a time. Anacaona wanted to go and see the "big canoe" of the white men. So she and her brother took a journey to the coast with Don Bartholomew. On the way they spent the night at a house where Anacaona kept all her treasures. They were things woven out of cotton, articles made of ebony and other kinds of woods, and utensils of clay, or of wood carefully carved. This Indian princess made presents out of her store to the white men. When the party reached the coast there were two painted canoes ready to carry Behechio and Anacaona to the ship. But Anacaona preferred to go in the ship's boat with Don Bartholomew. As they were being rowed out to the ship a salute was fired from a cannon on board. Anacaona fell over into the arms of Don Bartholomew, and the other Indians were on the point of jumping overboard. But the Spaniards laughed, and persuaded them out of their fright. Music now struck up on board the ship, and the fright of the Indians turned to delight. They wondered very much at everything they saw on shipboard. They were taken for a little sail, and watched the ship move by means of her sails with astonishment.

CHAPTER XXXV.

A REBELLION AND A WAR.
1497-1498.

It was much easier for Bartholomew Columbus to manage the savages than to control the Spaniards. They were mostly worthless men who hated him for a foreign upstart, and it seems certain that Don Bartholomew governed with a good deal of severity.

There was a man in the colony named Roldan, who had been made by Columbus *alcalde mayor*, or chief judge of Hispaniola—though he had come out as a servant. He became the leader of the many malcontents in the island. In the first place, he and his followers made a plot to kill Bartholomew at the execution of the Spaniard who had stolen the wife of Guarionex, this criminal having been a friend of Roldan's. As Bartholomew finally pardoned the fellow, the plot fell through.

When the caravel which brought the bread and cotton from Xaragua had been unloaded Don Bartholomew had her drawn up on shore, perhaps because he feared the malcontents would run away with her. The rebels demanded that the ship should be launched, and Bartholomew Columbus refused to launch her. So Roldan and seventy men presently marched out of Isabella and wandered about the country, making trouble with the Indians. Don Bartholomew dared not come to an open fight with them because of the discontent among his own men, who might at any moment desert him. Meanwhile the Indians at a distance took advantage of the troubles to leave off paying tribute, and

WELL AT SANTO DOMINGO, WHERE SHIPS GET WATER, SAID TO HAVE BEEN BUILT BY BARTHOLOMEW COLUMBUS.

Bartholomew Columbus thought best to excuse those who were near at hand, as he was afraid that they would join Roldan if he did not.

Ships arrived from Spain in February, 1498, with fresh soldiers and provisions. At this time Don Bartholomew was shut up in Fort Concepcion, with very little chance for getting food, and Roldan was about to

A REBELLION AND A WAR.

besiege him. The tables were turned when the ships arrived. Don Bartholomew took most of his troops over to Santo Domingo, Roldan and the rebels following. Bartholomew promised forgiveness to the rebels if they would return to duty, but perhaps Roldan did not believe that he would be forgiven. At any rate, he marched off with his men to Xaragua, which was thought to be a kind of paradise, since Bartholomew Columbus had been so well treated there.

The rebellion of Roldan had encouraged the Indians to make fresh trouble. Guarionex laid a plot with a number of other chiefs to surprise Fort Concepcion while Don Bartholomew was away. There were Spanish soldiers quartered around in the Indian villages, and it was agreed that while Guarionex took the fort the other chiefs were to fall upon these scattered parties and massacre them. As the Indians had no calendars, and were not good at counting, the night of the full moon was appointed for the attack. One chief, however, made a mistake about the moon, and took up arms one night too soon. The soldiers whom he attacked beat him, and, of course, the plan was spoiled. Guarionex put this chief to death for a blunder in astronomy.

Don Bartholomew was soon marching down upon the Vega. Guarionex did not wait for him, but fled with his family to the mountains of Ciquay. The Indians who lived in these mountains were a hardy tribe, and they had a chief named Mayobanex, who received the fugitive Guarionex. The mountain Indians now began to descend into the Vega, and massacre Spaniards or Indians friendly to the Spaniards. It would not do to let this sort of thing go on, so Don Bartholomew marched into the mountains, over a steep defile, and into a valley. There were, of course, Indian scouts on the watch to see where the white men were going. As the Spaniards were about to ford a river, they came upon two scouts in the bushes on its banks. One of them threw himself into the water and swam away. The other was caught, however, and forced to tell that there were thousands of Indians lying in ambush on the other shore. It was well for the white men that they were warned of this. The troops crossed where the water was shallow. When they were half way over the Indians sent showers of arrows and lances into their midst. In spite of their bucklers many Spaniards were wounded, but they pushed on and the enemy fled. On their way into the country they had to go more than once through Indian ambuscades.

Don Bartholomew sent one of the Indians of the country whom he had captured to Mayobanex, promising to make the chief no more trouble if he would give up Guarionex.

"Tell the Spaniards," said Mayobanex, "that they are bad men, cruel and tyrannical, usurpers of the lands of others and shedders of innocent blood. I do not want the friendship of such men. Guarionex is a good man, he is my friend, he has fled to me for refuge, I have promised to protect him and I will keep my word."

As it was impossible to find the Indians in order to fight them, Don Bartholomew began to burn their villages. The natives now begged their chief to give up Guarionex, but Mayobanex would not hear of this. He ordered men to lie in ambush and kill any messen-

Don Bartholomew finds his messengers dead.

gers that were sent to him with offers of peace from the white men. They presently killed two, one of whom was a member of their own tribe. When he saw his messengers shot through and through with arrows, Don Bartholomew was very angry. He marched to the home of the chief, only to find that he and Guarionex had both fled to the mountains.

The Spaniards had a pretty hard time of it, scrambling around among the mountains, living mostly on the little rabbits which their dogs hunted, and sleeping on the ground with the heavy tropical dew falling on them. Don Bartholomew finally dismissed most of his men who wished to attend to their farms in the Vega, and ranged the mountains with only thirty followers. He at length captured some Indians whom he forced to tell him where their chief was. Twelve Spaniards agreed to go and capture him. They took off their clothes and stained themselves to look like Indians. Wrapping their swords in palm leaves, they climbed to the hiding-place of Mayobanex. They surprised him and his family and took them captives to Fort Concepcion. The Indians of Ciquay presently came with presents begging for the release of their chief. Don Bartholomew freed his family, but kept him a prisoner to make sure of the good behavior of his people. As for Guarionex, he was finally caught when he descended into the Vega to look for food. Don Bartholomew was content to keep him a prisoner.

Meantime the rebels in Xaragua were having a fine time. One day they saw three ships off the coast. They were at first somewhat frightened, thinking that some one had come to capture them. But Roldan began to think that they might be ships which had been carried out of their course, and that the people in them were fresh from Spain and would not know anything about the rebellion, all of which was true enough, for they were the three ships that Columbus had sent from the Canaries. Roldan warned his men to keep quiet and went on board, telling the captains that he was stationed here to keep the natives down. He had no trouble in getting a good supply of arms from them, while his men took the chance to gain over the men on board the ships, who were mostly convicts, and easily persuaded to be lawless. When the captains of the ships found out, after three days, that they were dealing with rebels, they tried to persuade Roldan out of his wrong course. As the winds were contrary, they resolved to send many of the men by land to Santo Domingo. The men were no sooner landed, however, than they nearly all deserted their captain and went over to the rebels.

The ships made their way around to the settlement, leaving one of the sea-captains, named Caravajal, to treat with the rebels and try to persuade them to go back to duty. Caravajal did not succeed in doing anything with them, though he got Roldan to promise that he would go to Santo Domingo when Columbus arrived. Several rebels escorted Caravajal overland, and he got to Santo Domingo almost as soon as the ships did.

CHAPTER XXXVI.

COLUMBUS AND THE REBELS.
1498-1499.

Columbus was never to have any peace in his colony. Worn out by his troubles in Spain, where he had had to labor hard to save his good name, and wearied

CHAPEL CALLED COLUMBUS'S CHAPEL, NEAR SANTO DOMINGO.

by his long voyage and night watching on shipboard, he reached Hispaniola in August, 1498, to find the colony split into two parties, and to find, of course, that very little gold had been gathered amid all the troubles, while Spain clamored for the long-promised riches.

The admiral on his arrival by way of Paria was

not well pleased to hear that the rebels were likely soon to arrive in the neighborhood. As there were still many discontented men in the settlement, and as one of their chief complaints was that the Columbus brothers wished to keep men in the island for their own good, Columbus offered to all who wished to return free passage in the ships which were about to sail for Spain. In this way he thought that he would get rid of some of the most worthless and troublesome men.

Roldan and his followers presently arrived near Fort Concepcion, where one of the rebels owned a farm. They quartered themselves on this farm. Miguel Ballester, who was commander of the fort, went out to meet the rebels and offer them pardon, according to the orders of Columbus. Ballester was an old man, good, frank, and faithful. Roldan used very high language to him, and said that he had not come to treat for peace, but to demand the release of some Indian prisoners who had been encouraged by him to engage in the last war, and who were now to be sent to Spain as slaves.

Columbus was in a dilemma. He dared not undertake to fight the rebels, for he was uncertain of his own men. When he mustered the latter, only about seventy appeared, and of these many were not to be depended on. One was lame, another ill, some had friends among the rebels, and almost all had excuses. Columbus had kept the ships waiting in the harbor some time, hoping to send good news to Spain of the rebellion being over. The provisions were being used up, and the Indian prisoners, shut up in the holds of the vessels, were perishing from the heat. Columbus had to send an account of the rebellion and let the ships go. Roldan also sent his complaints to Spain.

The chief complaint of the rebels was against the severe government of Don Bartholomew. So Columbus wrote to them, begging them to submit to him, and promising full pardon. He sent this letter by Caravajal, for the rebels would have no other messenger. There was a great deal of clamor among them when the letter arrived. Some of the leaders got on their horses to go to Columbus, but the others would not let them go. At last they sent word to Columbus, asking for a written passport. This was given, and Roldan came to Santo Domingo, where he asked more than Columbus thought he could grant. In truth, the rebels wished to make very sure that they would not be punished, and also demanded large rewards for coming back to their duty. Roldan went away and was presently besieging Fort Concepcion, having cut off the water supply, pretending that he wanted an Indian who was in the fort. Columbus sent a proclamation, promising full forgiveness to any one who would return to duty in thirty days. When Caravajal posted the proclamation on the gate of the fort the rebels hooted at it. They thought better of besieging the fort, however, and agreed to come to terms if Columbus would give them each an Indian slave and send them back to Spain in the colony's two ships. Columbus had intended to send Bartholomew with these ships to the pearl coast to get more pearls, but he gave this up and promised to send the rebels to Spain. The latter marched off to Xaragua to wait for the ships.

After a good deal of time was taken up in getting

the vessels ready to sail, the rebels finally changed their minds and refused to go. Caravajal turned away from them disgusted, and started to return to Santo Domingo. Roldan rode with him a little way, and told him that if Columbus would send him a written passport he would come and treat with him. The passport was sent, and Roldan came to Santo Domingo. Columbus finally agreed to his demands, giving him property enough to make him a rich man, and putting him back in his office. Columbus had to bear a great deal from the recent rebels. To many of them he gave grants of lands and slaves from among the Indians captured in the wars, for in so short a time the Indians had come to this—their lands were not only divided among their conquerors, but they were themselves enslaved.

Columbus would have liked now to return to Spain, for he was, as he said, "absent, envied, and a stranger." But there were fresh troubles threatening, and he dared not leave. The next thing was the arrival of Alonzo de Ojeda, whose daring had once been so useful in the island. He had gone back to Spain, and, as he was a relative of Bishop Fonseca, who had control of Indian affairs, he had been allowed to sail to the coast of South America on a voyage of his own, having first seen a map made on the third voyage of Columbus, which the admiral had sent home to the king and queen. Ojeda had heard of the finding of pearls at Paria by Columbus, and had gone in search of them. He was now on his return, and, as he knew that Columbus would not like it that such an expedition should be sent out without his knowledge, Ojeda did not go to Santo Domingo, but stopped at the western part of Hispaniola to lay in

COLUMBUS AND THE REBELS. 215

dye-woods and a cargo of slaves without asking permission. On these ships were two of the old pilots of Columbus and the famous Amerigo Vespucci, who afterward wrote an account of his voyages, which happened to get him the undeserved honor of having the New World named after him.

Columbus hit upon the very good plan of sending Roldan to deal with Ojeda. It was a case of setting a rogue to catch a rogue, and worked very well, for Roldan was afraid that when his proceedings were known in Spain he might get into trouble if he did not do something to make his rebellion forgotten. He took two caravels and sailed along the coast to a place near that at which Ojeda had landed. He sent scouts ahead, and, finding that Ojeda was in an Indian village with a few of his men, who were making cassava bread, Roldan threw himself between Ojeda and his ships. Ojeda heard of this from the Indians, and, walking boldly up to Roldan, began to talk with him. Roldan asked him why he had landed on a lonely part of the island without reporting himself to the admiral. Ojeda answered that he had been on a voyage of discovery; that he was in distress, and had put in for provisions. Roldan asked to see the license that he sailed under. Ojeda said that his papers were on board the ships, and that he would sail around to Santo Domingo and report to the admiral. Roldan went on board the ships, saw the papers, and then went back to Columbus, who waited for Ojeda to come and see him.

Instead of this, Ojeda sailed around to Xaragua. Here he found some of Roldan's old followers, who made complaints to him of the Columbus brothers and of Roldan, who, they said, had deserted them. So Ojeda set up as their champion. He made bold to do this, because he knew that Columbus was not in very good favor at court, and that the queen, who was always the friend of Columbus, was ill. Ojeda prepared to march at the head of the rebels to Santo Domingo. Some were for going, some for staying, and there was a brawl in which several men were killed. The party for going gained the day, and the performances of Roldan were likely to be enacted over again, when Roldan himself appeared on the scene. Ojeda made haste to retire to the ships. Roldan then sent a letter to Ojeda, begging him in very good style not to go against law and order. He tried to get Ojeda to come ashore, but Ojeda would not. The two rogues distrusted one another. A one-armed sailor had deserted from the ships, and Ojeda seized two of Roldan's men in place of him.

Ojeda made sail to the north, landed in a beautiful country, and seized the food of the natives. Roldan and Escobar, who was also an old rebel, followed along shore. Roldan had thought of a very pretty little scheme. He sent Escobar in a canoe to within hailing distance of the ships to say that since Ojeda would not trust himself ashore, Roldan would come on board if a boat were sent for him. The boat was sent and lay a little off shore, the men saying that Roldan might come out to them, for they were afraid to land.

"How many may accompany me?" asked Roldan.

"Only five or six," answered the men in the boat.

So Escobar and four other men waded out and got into the boat. Roldan had to come yet, and, as he was a man of position, he must have a man to carry him out to the boat, and another to walk beside and help. By this trick he got to the boat eight strong. He got in and ordered the boat's crew to row ashore. They refused. Roldan and his men then drew their swords and attacked them, wounding several, and taking them all prisoners except an Indian, who swam away.

This was quite a blow to Ojeda, as he could not spare his boat, so he soon came to terms, returned the men he had captured, and agreed to leave the island if his men and boat were returned. He did not fail, however, to land at another of the West Indies and make up what he called his drove of Indian slaves.

It was not long before there was new trouble in the island. This time Columbus and Roldan were pitted against a man named Moxica, who had been one of the old rebels, and had been given lands as a reward for good behavior. Moxica and others planned to murder both Roldan and Columbus, and would perhaps have succeeded had not one of the rebels deserted and revealed the plot. Columbus meant to nip this rebellion in the bud. With nine or ten men he went secretly in the night and captured the ringleaders. He resolved to hang Moxica on the top of Fort Concepcion. Moxica was allowed first to confess, but the fellow was a coward, and when the priest came he tried to prolong his life by delaying his confession and accusing others. In a passion Columbus caused him to be thrown over the battlements. He afterward executed others of the leaders of this rebellion.

CHAPTER XXXVII.

THE KING AND QUEEN DISPLEASED.
1500.

In Spain there had been nothing but bad news from Hispaniola. Seven years had passed since Columbus had sailed to the New World, his over-hopeful imagination leading him to promise riches so vast that he had thought by this time to have furnished from his own purse an army to rescue the sepulchre of Christ from the Mohammedans. But gold had only been eked out in small quantities, and the colony had been a great expense to the sovereigns. Most of the people who had returned from Hispaniola were those whose worthlessness and unruliness in the colony had made it necessary to get rid of them. Of course, these had sad tales to tell about the new land and many complaints to make of the government of the Columbus brothers, though they easily forgot to mention their own sins.

There were people at court who envied Columbus and who talked about his not being a Spaniard, which was a great crime in their eyes. The Spanish grandees were the proudest gentlemen in the world, and the fact that Columbus and his brothers were of humble birth made them hateful in their eyes. It was even suggested that this foreigner would some day make himself an independent king of Hispaniola.

Beside the complaint sent by Roldan, there were the letters of Columbus himself, in which he had written about the rebellion of Roldan, and asked for some one to be sent out to settle the dispute between him and the rebels. It was natural that the king and queen should think that Columbus was not a very good governor. There is no doubt but that he was an unpopular one. Ferdinand and Isabella decided to send some one out to inquire into the troubles of the colony, and remove Columbus from the government should it be necessary. But they waited a year before they did this. Meantime the queen, who had always been the particular friend of Columbus, was displeased with him because he kept sending Indian slaves to Spain. Many of the followers of Roldan had exacted when they submitted that they should be returned to Spain and allowed to take some slaves with them. Some of these men had brought back native "princesses" or chiefs' daughters, whom they had coaxed away from their homes. Many of these Indian women had babies with them, who were the children of their masters. The queen was very angry at this scandal.

"What right," said she, "has my viceroy to give away my subjects to such ends?"

When the king and queen rode out they were besieged by miserable wretches returned from the New World, who cried:

"Pay! Pay!" demanding pay for their services.

Once about fifty of these beggars seated themselves near the palace of the Alhambra, in Granada, and bought a load of grapes which they divided up and began to eat. When the king and queen passed they held up bunches of grapes, and cried that they were reduced to live on such food because Columbus had not paid them their due. Grapes, of course, were plentiful in southern Spain; in other lands this might not have seemed very cheap living.

When Diego and Ferdinand Columbus, who were pages to the queen, passed near these fellows, they would say to one another, quite loud enough to be heard: "There are the sons of the admiral of Mosquitoland, who has discovered the land of deceit and disappointment, to make Spanish gentlemen die of misery there."

Even a king and queen could not stand so much importunity. So a man named Francisco de Bobadilla was sent out to Hispaniola to investigate matters. If affairs were found in a bad state, he was authorized to take the government away from Columbus. The queen also sent some of the Indian slaves back to their homes.

CHAPTER XXXVIII.

COLUMBUS IN CHAINS.

1500.

Eight years after his great discovery of the New World came the darkest days in the life of Columbus. It must be admitted that he seems to have been a rather harsh ruler, and that his men had some cause for complaint on this score; but, on the other hand, he had very difficult and lawless men to deal with. It is hard at this distance to tell whether a foreigner like Columbus could have done any better with a Spanish colony. When Bobadilla arrived in August of the year 1500, Columbus had just caused several of the rebels, whose leader he had thrown from the top of a fort, to be hanged. The first thing that Bobadilla saw when he went ashore was two men hanging from gibbets. He naturally concluded that Columbus was indeed cruel. Of course all who were discontented were quick to carry their complaints to him, and it did not take long for Bobadilla to decide that it was necessary for him to take the office of governor himself, especially as he was a needy man. He attacked the fortress, followed by a mob carrying scaling ladders. The rabble having broken down the door, the garrison of two men speedily surrendered. Bobadilla also took possession of the house of Columbus, with all the gold which belonged to the admiral as his share of the profits from the mines and all the books and papers of the great discoverer. To make himself popular he paid the salaries

TOWER IN WHICH IT IS SAID COLUMBUS WAS IMPRISONED.

overdue out of this gold and allowed the colonists various liberties, one of which was the privilege of looking for gold and paying only one eleventh to the crown instead of one third, as before.

When the news reached Columbus at Fort Concepcion of what Bobadilla had done, he thought at first that it was the deed of some adventurer like Ojeda. When Bobadilla sent him word to surrender, he refused, saying that the government of the island had been granted to him for life, and that no one could take it away from him. But when a letter of credence was brought to him signed "I, the King" and "I, the

COLUMBUS IN CHAINS.

Queen," commanding him to obey Bobadilla, he set out at once for Santo Domingo almost alone. When he came quietly into the town, Bobadilla ordered him to be put in irons. The chains were brought, but no one wanted to rivet them on the legs of the great discoverer. At last one of his own servants, "a graceless and shameless cook," consented to put the irons on his master. This fellow, "with unwashed front," as the old story says, fastened the irons on Columbus, "quite as though he were serving him with some choice dish."

Diego Columbus was also put in irons and Bartholomew, who was in Xaragua, punishing some of the rebels, was sent for. Columbus wrote to him to deliver himself up peaceably. The three brothers were imprisoned, Christopher in the fortress and Diego and Bartholomew on board vessels in the harbor, so that they might not communicate with one another. For

INTERIOR OF THE FORTRESS IN WHICH IT IS SUPPOSED COLUMBUS WAS IMPRISONED.

two months Columbus lay in prison in the tower of Santo Domingo, which still stands to-day. By this time Bobadilla had made out a great many charges against him, the end of which he thought would justify his own conduct. A gentleman named Alonzo de Villejo was now commanded to take the Columbus brothers to Spain.

During his two months of lonely imprisonment the great discoverer had fallen into despair. He did not know what Bobadilla might not do next. When Villejo came for him with a guard, he thought that perhaps his last moment had come.

"Villejo," he said, sadly, "whither are you taking me?"

"To the ship, your excellency, to embark."

"To embark!" exclaimed Columbus. "Villejo, do you speak the truth?"

"By the life of your excellency, it is true," said Villejo.

Columbus was greatly comforted, and seemed like one restored from death to life.

After they were out to sea the gentlemanly Villejo and the captain of the ship wanted to take the disgraceful irons off of the great man.

"No," answered Columbus, "their majesties commanded me to submit to whatever Bobadilla should order in their name. I will wear these chains until they shall order them to be taken off, and I will keep them afterward as memorials of the reward of my services."

CHAPTER XXXIX.

COLUMBUS LANDS IN CHAINS.
1500.

When the discoverer landed at Cadiz in chains there was a great reaction of sympathy for him and much indignation. So long as he was fancied to be the rich viceroy of the Indies, while his men came home gaunt and discontented, people were wont to pity the poor colonists and blame Columbus; but when the finder of a new world was seen loaded with chains, there was general disgust that a great man should be treated in this way.

After he landed, Columbus wrote a letter to Donna Juana de la Torre, a lady who was a favorite of Queen Isabella, and had been nurse to Prince Juan. Columbus apparently dared not write directly to the king or queen, but he expected that this letter would be shown to them. It was a very sad letter. He said in it: "I have now reached a point that there is no man so vile but thinks it his right to insult me. The day will come when the world will reckon it a virtue to him who has not given his consent to their abuse." He told how wicked many of the colonists were. "If their highnesses," he said, "would cause a general inquiry to be made throughout the land, I assure you that they would be astonished that the island has not been swallowed up." Columbus then alludes to the report that he had been accused of wishing to take the Indies away from Spain. "I do not imagine," he says, "that any one supposed me so stupid as not to be aware that even if the Indies had belonged to me I could not support myself without the assistance of some prince. In such case, where should I find a better support or more security against expulsion than in the king and queen, our sovereigns?" He also told how Bobadilla had seized the gold, among which were some rich pieces of ore as big as a goose's egg and some pearls which he had been saving to take to the king and queen; how he had taken it without weighing it, had used some of it to pay the men whose wages were overdue, and had kept the rest to "feather his own nest" with.

"I have been wounded extremely," said Columbus, "that a man should have been sent out to make inquiry into my conduct who knew that if he sent home an aggravated account of the result of his investigation he would remain at the head of the government." The rest of the letter is devoted to proving that gold was now being found in abundance in the island, for Columbus, after he had made his discoveries, was ever put to trouble to prove their value in European eyes. He said that the road was now "open to gold and pearls, and it may surely be hoped that precious stones, spices, and a thousand other things will also be found." We know that Columbus had indeed opened the road for a great deal of riches for Spain, though he was to be in his grave before they began to flow in very great quantities; and we also know that the road was open for many other benefits to the Old World, though they

COLUMBUS LANDS IN CHAINS.

would not be precisely the spices and other things for which it looked.

When the queen heard how Columbus had been sent home in chains, she was greatly shocked. The king and queen immediately sent orders to Cadiz that the Columbus brothers should be set free and treated with distinction. They also sent Christopher Columbus a letter in which they told him how grieved they were at the way in which he had been treated, and asked him to come to court.

Columbus went to court. When the queen saw him, her kind eyes filled with tears. This was too much for Columbus. He threw himself on his knees at her feet, weeping and sobbing. He had a long talk with the sovereigns, and they made him fair promises, so that he was somewhat comforted.

CHAPTER XL.

COLUMBUS UNDER A CLOUD.
1500–1502.

Though the king and queen received him well, and showed sorrow for the unjust treatment he had undergone, they did not really take Columbus back into favor. It was nearly a year before an order was given that the property which Bobadilla had seized should be returned, and his eighth of the revenue paid him. Meantime Columbus was poor, and under a sort of disgrace. His right to govern the lands he had discovered and to an interest in the voyages made to the New World, as well as the descent of the honors in his family, seemed likely all to be lost. He was again a poor man, begging favors of the Spanish court, and being put off from time to time. This was very unjust, for the great ideas and the noble perseverance of Columbus had given to the Spanish crown lands many times larger than the whole of Spain.

While Columbus had been away struggling with his unhappy colony, or coming home in chains, a great deal had happened in the world of discovery. The Portuguese, after so many years, had carried out Prince Henry's scheme of sailing around Africa and so reaching India. Vasco da Gama had arrived at Calcutta at the same time that Columbus was setting out on his third voyage, in which he discovered the main-land of South America. Vasco da Gama found at Calcutta most of the treasures for which Columbus had looked so eagerly in the New World. The Rajah of Calcutta sent a letter to the King of Portugal, which read: "Vasco da Gama, a nobleman of your household, has visited my kingdom, which has given me great pleasure. In my kingdom there is an abundance of cinnamon, cloves, ginger, pepper, and precious stones in great quantities. What I seek from thy country is gold, silver, coral, and scarlet." Da Gama returned from his long voyage, having lost half his vessels and more than half his men, but he was hailed with great joy in Portugal.

PORTRAIT OF VASCO DA GAMA, FROM A MANUSCRIPT OF HIS TIME.

While Columbus was struggling with his rebellious colony, the Portuguese had sent out a fine fleet of thirteen vessels to again make the voyage to India. They sailed far west to avoid the coast of Africa, where there were calms, and the fleet was blown by a storm to the very shores of the New World. As Brazil, where they landed, was east of the line within which the Pope had allowed Portugal to make discoveries, the Portuguese made haste to claim this new land. It has been said that this accidental discovery of the New World by the Portuguese proves that America would soon have been found if Columbus had never had his noble idea of sailing westward. Perhaps, however, the Portuguese seamen would not have ventured any farther to the west than they had done before if Columbus had not first dared to sail straight out into the boundless ocean. At least, it is far more interesting that the discovery should have been made by a man who thought it out first, and overcame so many obstacles to accomplish it.

Of course, the court of Spain was jealous of the Portuguese discoveries, just as the Portuguese court had been jealous of the discoveries of Columbus. The finding of Brazil by Portugal, and the finding of North America by Cabot for England, made King Ferdinand anxious to make settlements in the New World as rapidly as he could, lest other powers should grasp too much of these vast lands which were coming to light. The Spanish court was poor, and could not afford alone to push Spanish discoveries very far. So a license had been granted for Spaniards to fit out ships at their own expense. In this way the crown was sure of a share in the profits without taking a share in the expense, though the rights of Columbus were left out of the account.

The result had been that there were several expeditions sent out to the New World after Columbus sent word of the discovery of pearls. In these voyages sailed those who had been old captains under Columbus, such as the Pinzons, and pilots who had been with him on his different voyages. One at least of these ships brought back a rich load of gold and pearls.

King Ferdinand probably thought that Columbus was not a good governor. Perhaps the plans which he cherished for the recovery of the Holy Sepulchre and the notions he held about the Garden of Eden and the mines of Solomon made him seem to the king a visionary. At any rate, Ferdinand appears to have been sorry

RUINS OF ST. NICHOLAS CHURCH, SANTO DOMINGO.

that he had given Columbus privileges so vast, and he was resolved to evade these obligations of his when it was possible.

Bobadilla had managed as badly as possible at Hispaniola. Under the privileges which he had rashly granted when he first landed, the colonists gave themselves up to all sorts of disorders. As he had allowed them to gather gold and pay only one eleventh to the crown, he was anxious that as much gold should be gathered as possible, in order that the crown should not lose by it. So the Indian chiefs were made to furnish slaves to work in the mines and in the fields. The seeds of slavery which had been planted in the days of Columbus were growing fast. The Indians were cruelly treated, and as they were not a hardy race they died off rapidly. Worthless Spaniards, who had been criminals at home, took on the airs of grand gentlemen. When they traveled they were carried by Indians in their hammocks, with slaves to hold palm-leaves over their heads and fan them with feather fans. Meantime the unhappy porters had their shoulders bleeding from carrying the ropes of the hammocks across them.

King Ferdinand appointed Nicholas de Ovando to govern the colony in place of Bobadilla. This governor was to reform abuses, require one third of the gold found, and check the growing evil of slavery, only forcing Indians to work for the crown, and paying them. With Ovando, the first negro slaves were permitted to be taken out to the New World, and so slavery was firmly planted in these beautiful tropical lands; for Indian slavery, having once been allowed, could never be rooted out until the weakly race had perished under its severities, while the negroes, who were a much hardier people, would speedily take the place of the natives.

Ovando was sent to Hispaniola in a fleet of thirty ships, with everything that could be needed for the colony. The new governor was allowed to dress in silks, brocades, and precious stones, in order to appear the

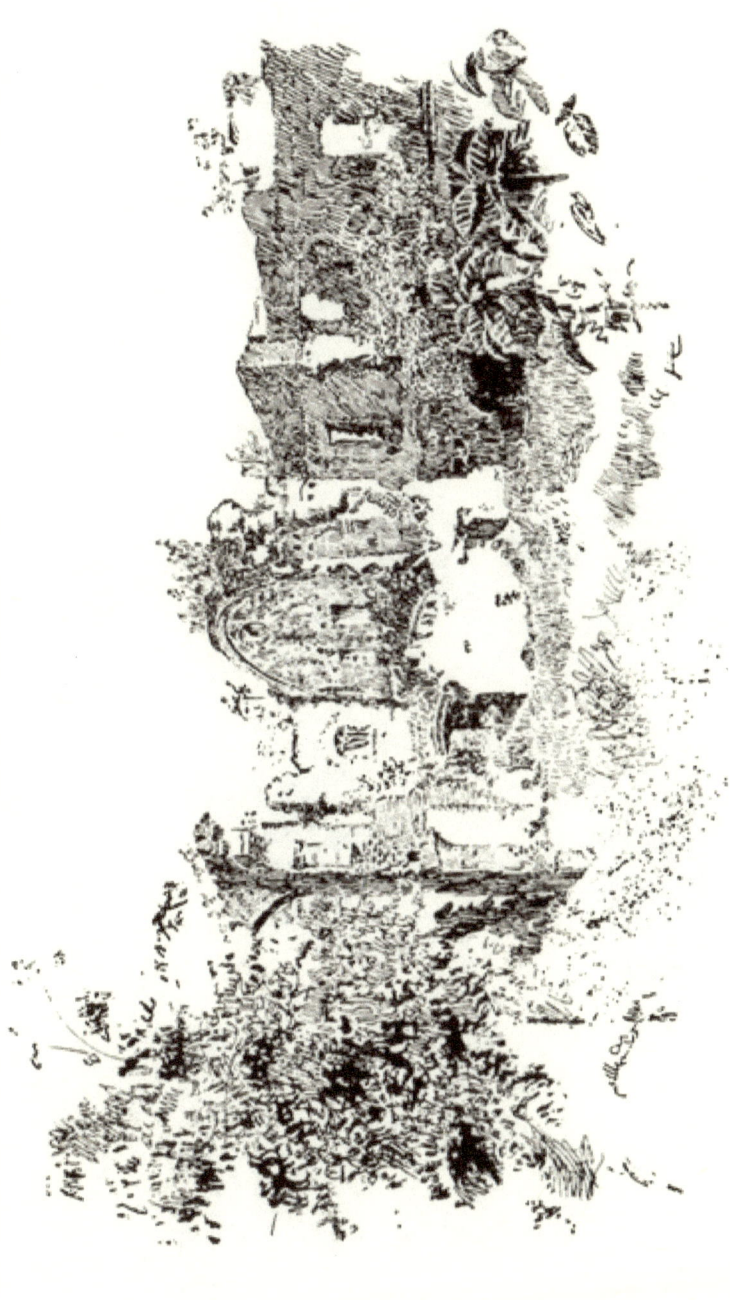

Interior of Dominican convent, Santo Domingo.

more dignified. This kind of dress was forbidden in Spain, because the nobility were extravagant. Governments were much given to meddling in matters of dress in those days.

Soon after Ovando sailed there was a terrible storm, the fleet was scattered, and the shores were strewed with things washed over from the ships. When this news reached Ferdinand and Isabella they shut themselves up for eight days, and gave way to grief, but they were comforted when it was found that only one ship had been lost.

Columbus must have thought it hard that Ovando was sent to Hispaniola so much better provided than he had ever been; but the king and queen promised him that they would restore him to the government of the island when the troubles there should have had time to subside. The mind of the great discoverer was now more than ever filled with his dream of rescuing the Holy Sepulchre. He wrote a long paper to convince the king and queen that this was the thing that they should do. Columbus wished to undertake another voyage to the New World, with the idea that he could find a strait somewhere that should lead through the lands already found to the Eastern countries, which, in the notions of that day, lay just beyond; but what Columbus thought most about was finding riches enough to carry out his plan of conquering Jerusalem from the infidel.

The great discoverer was allowed four little ships for his voyage. It was agreed that he was to go to an undiscovered part of the New World, and was not to touch at Hispaniola on his outward voyage.

Before Columbus sailed once more for the New World, he put all his papers in careful order. As he considered that he might never come back from this voyage, he made arrangements for the distribution of his property. One of his plans was to leave one tenth of his revenue, if it should ever come to amount to anything, to the Bank of St. George, in Genoa, to be used to reduce the tax on corn, wine, and other provisions. It is evident that Columbus remembered his native city with affection, and generously wished to lift a little of the burden of taxation off of plain people, such as his own family had been.

CHAPTER XLI.

COLUMBUS PREDICTS A HURRICANE.
1502.

Columbus set sail on his fourth voyage to the new world on the 9th of May, 1502, nearly three months after Ovando had sailed for Hispaniola. He took with him his brother Bartholomew and his younger son, Ferdinand, who was not quite fourteen years old. He made a quick passage, and on the 15th of June sighted one of the Caribbee Islands called Mantinino, or Martinico, as it is now called. The ships stopped at this island for three days, taking in wood and water, while the men washed their clothes. The admiral sailed next to the Island of Dominica; from there to Santa Cruz and along the south side of Porto Rico. He had meant to go to Jamaica and from there to the continent, but one of his ships was a very bad sailer and could not carry much canvas, and he wished to exchange her for another vessel or buy one outright. So he steered for his old home at Hispaniola, though he had been forbidden to do this.

At the time when Columbus neared Santo Domingo Ovando had been in the island for about two months, had taken the government away from Bobadilla, had made a strict investigation of the conduct of Roldan and the other rebels, and had caused many of them to be arrested, in order to be sent to Spain for trial. The fleet in which Ovando had come out was about to sail on the return voyage when Columbus appeared. A great deal of gold, which had been gathered by Bobadilla during his government, was loaded on the largest ship, in which Bobadilla himself was to sail. There was one nugget weighing thirty-six hundred castellanos, which had been found by an Indian woman in a brook. Her Spanish masters are said to have dined on roast pig, served on this piece of gold. In this ship was to sail also the chief Guarionex, who had been a prisoner all this time. Roldan and those of his followers who were arrested, as well as others, put their gold into different vessels of the fleet. One ship was loaded by the agent of Columbus with his share of the treasure, which amounted to four thousand pieces of gold.

CEIBA TREE, TO WHICH IT IS SAID THE SHIPS MOORED IN COLUMBUS' TIME.

It was the 29th of June, and the richly laden fleet was about to set sail when Columbus arrived. He sent one of his captains on shore, asking that he might get a ship in exchange for the one which sailed badly, and also begging that he might be allowed to take shelter in the harbor, for he thought that a storm was coming. But Ovando refused. Perhaps he may have feared that some injury might be done to the discoverer, since Santo Domingo was at that time full of his enemies, who were very angry because so many of their friends had been arrested. Columbus sent the captain back once more to Ovando, begging him not to let the fleet sail for several days, as there was a storm coming. But Ovando paid no heed to the warning of the discoverer, and the fleet sailed, putting directly out to sea. Columbus left the harbor also, driven away from the shores he had discovered. His men grumbled because they had sailed with an admiral who was treated in this way.

Columbus had not seen the hurricanes of the tropical countries without observing the signs of them. He hugged the shore of the island, as he expected the storm would come from the land side. In two days the hurricane came. It was a terrible storm. The fleet of Bobadilla was scattered hither and thither. Several ships went to the bottom. Bobadilla, Roldan, and some of the worst enemies of Columbus, as well as the chief Guarionex, and the great mass of gold and other riches, were swallowed up in the ocean. It was a kind of case of poetic justice, for it is even said that the only ship which was able to sail on for Spain was the one on which the gold belonging to Columbus was put.

It was a fearful time for the fleet of Columbus. The ships weathered the first day, under shelter of the land. The next day the storm was worse than ever, and the vessels lost sight of each other. Columbus, according to his first plan, still hugged the shore, but the others ran out for sea-room at night. Don Bartholomew, who commanded the poorest ship, barely escaped shipwreck At last they all got together in a wild bay. The vessels which had run out to sea were more or less injured, while Columbus had lost his long boat.

When the news reached Santo Domingo that the enemies of Columbus had been ingulfed, while he was safe, there were men who said that Columbus had brought about this storm by magic, in order to revenge himself on Bobadilla. In those days, a man of more knowledge than the common was likely to be suspected of dealings with evil spirits.

CHAPTER XLII.

COLUMBUS AT HONDURAS.

1502.

Columbus had no sooner put out of harbor than he was forced back by a fresh storm. At last he made a start, and sailed to some little islands near Jamaica, where the men got fresh water by digging holes in the sand. There was a calm, and the currents carried the ships over to the coast of Cuba, where were the keys that had been called the Queen's Garden. A favorable wind presently began to blow, and Columbus struck out for fresh discoveries, sailing southwest from Cuba. He reached the main-land in the province of Honduras. The admiral sent his brother Bartholomew ashore. The people seemed to be much like the Indians they had seen before, except that their foreheads were a little larger. The sailors discovered a good deal of copper here, which they took for gold and gathered greedily, trying to hide it when they went on shipboard, so that it would not be taken from them for the crown.

While Bartholomew Columbus was ashore a great canoe arrived from some other country. This boat was made of a single tree-trunk, but was eight feet wide and very long. In the middle of it was a cabin, so thickly covered with palm-leaves as to keep out rain and seawater. Under this cabin were women and children.

The boat was paddled by twenty-five men. These Indians did not offer any resistance, but allowed themselves to be captured by the white men. The women were wrapped in cotton mantles, and the men wore cotton cloths about their middle. They were somewhat better clothed than any Indians found in the New World before. It is thought that this canoe came from Yuca-

MAP OF COLUMBUS' LAST VOYAGE OF DISCOVERY.

tan, where the people, who lived on the border of Mexico, were more civilized than elsewhere. The boat was probably on a trading voyage. It was loaded with all kinds of Indian goods. There were sleeveless cotton garments, embroidered or dyed in various colors, aprons of cotton such as the Indians wore, and mantles of cotton cloth. Then there were copper hatchets and wooden swords, which had grooves cut in each side, in which sharp pieces of flint were tied by cords made of the intestines of fish. This kind of weapon was afterward found among the Mexicans and in Virginia. There were also utensils made of clay, stone, or hard wood, and a great many cacao-nuts. The Spaniards had not yet been introduced to the drink called chocolate, which was made out of this nut. They noticed that when an Indian let one of the cacao-nuts drop, he picked it up in as much haste as though he had lost an eye out of his head. The fact is that the Indians used the cacao-nuts for money, and this is why they were so afraid of losing one. Columbus selected what he thought most interesting from the goods of these people, and, having paid them in trinkets, he set them free, all but an old man, whom he kept for a guide.

When asked where they came from, these Indians had pointed toward the west. If he had sailed west and north, Columbus might have discovered the empire of Mexico, but he turned eastward. He was looking for a strait which should lead to India, and expected to find it by sailing toward Paria. The admiral did, indeed, sail to where the two great continents were joined by a narrow isthmus, which was the nearest approach to a strait. The fact seems to be that Columbus asked the Indians where there was a strait, and they pointed toward Panama; but the white men and natives did not understand each other very well, and the Indians meant a strait of land—that is, an isthmus. Columbus hoped to press through the strait and so reach a sort of middle sea like the Mediterranean, which should quickly lead to India. Of course, he had no dream of such an immense ocean as the Pacific. Had there been a strait, Columbus would probably have tried to go around the world, and would have perished of hunger if he had not turned back. Long after he was dead, discoverers were still looking for a passage through the American continent. The Isthmus of Panama is a very inconvenient affair, and the strait is still so much wanted that in our day two canals have been undertaken, with a view of getting through from ocean to ocean.

Bartholomew Columbus landed at Cape Honduras on the 14th of August and said mass. Again he landed at a river which he called the River of Possession, because he took possession of the country here in the usual style. The Indians of this place brought food and laid it at the feet of Don Bartholomew, and then moved away without saying anything. Bartholomew offered them little beads and bells, which they came and took; but when he tried to talk with them he could not make them understand, even with the help of the old interpreter. The next day these Indians brought fowls, eggs, roasted fish, red and white beans, and other Indian food, to the white men.

The Spaniards noticed that the natives of this coast made a sort of cuirass of quilted cotton to protect themselves from arrows. In one place the people were very dark, and the old interpreter assured them that these savage-looking fellows ate human flesh. These Indians heightened their ill-looks by slitting their ears and stretching them by some means, so that the slit alone was large enough to pass an egg through. The Spaniards named this region La Costa de la Oreja, or the Coast of the Ear.

The ships made their way, hindered by contrary currents and frequent storms, along a low but beautiful shore. The people were almost entirely naked, though some of them wore a sort of sleeveless shirt. Their bodies were tattooed or otherwise bedizened with the figures of animals and Indian cabins, which produced a curious effect. The most important men among them wore pieces of white and red cotton on the head, or tresses of hair hanging down in front. On dress occasions they painted their faces black or red, or streaked them with lines of various colors, while some were content with blacking around their eyes. When these savages thought themselves the finest, the white men were of the opinion that they looked very much like devils.

For some two months Columbus struggled along the coast of the new continent, opposed by contrary currents and incessant storms. Sometimes the tempest was so frightful that it seemed as though the end of the world had come, and the terrified sailors confessed their sins to one another. The

INDIAN FIGURE OF STONE FOUND ON THE HONDURAS COAST.

ships grew more and more leaky, the sails were torn, and the provisions were hurt by being mixed with sea or rain water. Columbus fell ill of the gout. He had a small cabin built on the stern of his ship, and here he lay in his bed and kept a lookout. Sometimes he was so ill that he expected soon to die. At such times he was anxious about his brother Bartholomew, who had not wanted to come on this voyage, and about little Ferdinand. Then he would think of Diego, whom he had left in Spain, and wonder whether he would ever manage to regain the rights which he had worked so hard to leave him. As for the boy Ferdinand, among all the trials of the voyage he was as steady as a man of eighty, as his father said, taking in with boyish interest all that he saw.

At last the ships doubled a cape, and the sailors found that the land turned suddenly southward, while the wind was with them. Columbus and his men were joyful at the change, and named the cape Gracias a Dios, or Thanks to God. At this point they set ashore their good old interpreter, loaded with presents, for they had come to a region where he no longer understood the speech of the natives.

CHAPTER XLIII.

MAGIC POWDER AND GOLD PLATES.

1502.

The ships sailed south along what is to-day called the Mosquito Coast. In the rivers were reeds, some of them as thick as a man's leg, and many alligators. At one place there were twelve small islands, which Columbus called the Limonares, because they were covered with lime-trees, and the limes seemed to Columbus much like lemons.

The vessels had sailed a long distance, and the men were in want of water. Two boats were sent up a river to get it. As they came back they were caught in a swelling of the sea caused by the waves rushing against the river current. One boat was overturned, and all on board were drowned. The sailors, who had already had a hard time of it, were disheartened by this accident. Columbus called the stream the River of Disaster.

After several days the admiral thought to give his men a rest, so he anchored between a little island and the main-land. The little island sent off a very sweet smell. There were many fruits growing on it, among which were bananas. On the main-land was a beautiful hilly country, with trees so high that they seemed to reach to the sky. The Indians, however, were unfriendly, and got together on the shore well armed and ready for a fight. But the white men did not try to land. They calmly rested on deck or busied themselves drying the wet provisions. Seeing that the strange beings were so peaceable, the Indians presently began to wave cotton mantles on the shore by way of inviting the white men to land. After a while they grew bold, and swam out to the ships with mantles and sleeveless shirts of cotton, and ornaments made of the mixed gold called quanin.

Columbus tried a new plan with these Indians. He would not take anything from them, but gave them trinkets, thinking that he would make an impression on them by being very generous. It seems to have made them suspicious, however, for when they got ashore they tied together all the things that the white men had given them and left them on the beach. No doubt they thought that there was something magical about these men, and were afraid of their gifts.

Some of the Spaniards one day went cautiously ashore to get water. When the boat was about to land an old Indian came out from the trees with a white cloth tied to the end of a stick as a sign of peace. He led two little Indian girls, who had ornaments of quanin hanging from their necks One of these girls was about fourteen and the other about eight years old. The old man brought them to the Spaniards, and seemed to want them to keep the girls as hostages. So the Spaniards went ashore and filled their water-barrels, while the Indians kept at a distance, and took pains not to frighten the strangers by any movements. When the Spaniards started to leave, the old man made signs

Sea-view and Indians of the Mosquito coast.

that they were to take the girls with them. So the two little Indian girls were taken on board the admiral's ship. After they had been feasted they were sent ashore, but as it was now dark, and their friends were gone, they were brought back again and spent the night on shipboard, where Columbus was very careful that the rough sailors did them no harm. They were sent back the next morning, and their friends received them joyfully. The same day, when the boats went ashore once more, the girls came with crowds of other Indians to return the presents that had been made to them on the ships.

The next day Don Bartholomew started to go ashore. Before his boat reached the land two Indians waded out into the water, and, taking him out of the boat, carried him on land and sat him down upon a grassy bank. Bartholomew Columbus began to question the Indians about their country. He ordered a notary who was with him to write down what was understood to be their answers. The notary, getting out pen, inkhorn, and paper, began to write. This was too much for the Indians, who thought this the performance of some spell, and fled in all directions. They presently returned, throwing a fragrant powder from a safe distance and burning some of it so that the smoke should blow toward the white men. The Spaniards were now disconcerted in their turn, for Europeans were almost as superstitious in those days as were the Indians. They began to think that these people were sorcerers. They thought they knew now why they had been retarded so much in sailing along these coasts. No doubt some spell had been worked by the witchcraft of the Indians. Even Columbus said that the people of Cariari, as this region was called, were great enchanters, and thought that the Indian girls who had come on board the ship had magic powder hidden about them.

In spite of the dreaded magic powder, Bartholomew Columbus made several trips ashore well protected, not by magic amulets but by good Spanish arms. He found nothing but quanin among the natives, but they told him that farther on he would find gold. He went into one of the Indian villages, and found in a large house some sepulchres. In these were bodies wrapped in cotton cloth and so embalmed that there was no bad odor from them. The corpses were dressed in their savage ornaments, and the sepulchres were adorned with rude carvings and paintings.

Before he left, Columbus had seven of the people seized. From them he selected two whom he thought the most intelligent, and let the others go. The Indians on shore were greatly distressed at this, and sent presents to the white men, begging for the release of their friends. Columbus tried to explain that he wanted them for guides, but they probably did not understand this, and perhaps wished that they had used more magic powder.

Columbus next sailed along a shore which has since been called Costa Rica, or Rich Coast, on account of the gold and silver mines which were afterward found here. He then entered the lagoons of Chiriqui, through a deep, narrow channel, where the rigging brushed against the branches of the trees which hung over the water. The Spaniards landed on one of the islands here. The Indian guides, whom Columbus had stolen from the land of magic powder, encouraged the natives of this island to come and trade with the whites. These people had large pieces of pure gold hanging by cotton cords around their necks. One of them sold a plate worth ten ducats, or about twenty dollars, for three little hawksbells.

The Spaniards made a second visit to the main-land the next day. Ten canoe-loads of Indians met them, adorned with flowers, and coronets made of the claws of animals and quills of birds. These Indians wore around their necks large plates of gold, hammered thin and burnished, but refused to sell them. The Spaniards captured two of them to carry off as guides. One of them wore a gold plate, and another an eagle made of gold.

In spite of the gold which Columbus found at Chiriqui, he hurried on eastward in search of the strait for which he was looking. As was always the case when Columbus tried to talk with the Indians by signs, he had got hold of a strange story. This time it was about a land in the interior where the people were rich and civilized, having ships, guns, and horses. This country was surrounded by the sea, while the river Ganges was thereabouts. Columbus thought that this desirable country must be on the other side of the land where he now was, which was, perhaps, a great peninsula like Spain. He expected soon to find an opening like the strait of Gibraltar, through which he would pass and reach some Eastern country, belonging perhaps to the Empire of the Grand Khan.

The next stopping-place of Columbus was at the mouth of a large river on the coast of Veragua. Some of the Spaniards rowed to land in the ships' boats.

About two hundred Indians assembled on the shore, armed for a fight, and kept up a lively din with wooden drums and conch-shells. As the boats neared land, the savages ran out into the sea up to their middles, splashing the water to show their fury. The Spaniards made signs of peace, however, and the natives were presently pacified, and consented to trade. Seventeen plates of gold were bought this day. The next day, when the sailors went back again, the Indians were as fierce as ever, rushing forward to the sound of

CHARACTERISTIC INDIAN BUILDING OF THE COAST.

drum and conch-shell, determined upon a battle. A cross-bow was fired at them, and wounded a savage in the arm. The Indians were quieted by this, but when a cannon was fired from one of the ships they all fled. Four Spaniards ran after them, calling to them to come back. They threw down their arms meekly enough, and brought three plates of gold as an offering to the white men.

The ships sailed on along the coast of Veragua and stopped again at another river. Here also there was a great noise of drums and conch-shells, and the savages were soon in battle array. Presently a canoe came off to the ships with two men in it. They talked with the interpreters, and were soon persuaded to go on board. They returned satisfied to the shore, so the Spaniards landed. Here they found a naked king among naked subjects. The only mark of distinction which this chief allowed himself was the having a very large leaf held over his head while it rained. He and his people exchanged nineteen large plates of gold for trinkets. The Spaniards found in this place some sort of a solid building, the first seen in the New World. Columbus kept a piece of the stone and lime of which it was made to carry back with him. This was probably one of the structures the ruins of which are still to be seen in parts of Central America.

CHAPTER XLIV.

BACK TO THE LAND OF GOLD.
1502-1503.

The ships ran by a number of towns where the guides said there was gold, but the wind was so very fresh that Columbus did not stop. His next anchorage was in a harbor which he called Puerto Bello, or Beautiful Port. Instead of being surrounded by forests, this bay had open country about it. There were many Indian houses standing in groves of fruit trees, while between them lay fields of corn, vegetables, and pineapples. This looked something like the fields and orchards of the Old World, and was a refreshing sight to homesick men. The Spaniards stayed seven days at Puerto Bello, because there were heavy rains and storms. The Indians brought them fruits, vegetables, and balls of cotton, but there was not much gold in this country, for only a few chiefs had some pieces hanging from their noses.

The admiral sailed on eastward from here, but he did not go very much farther. Indeed, one of the Spanish ships which had recently made a voyage to these parts had explored about as far as this from the other direction, though we are not sure whether Columbus knew this. At any rate, he began to give up the strait that he wished for so much, though he did not know that he had just coasted the shore of the great isthmus. It had taken four months to explore as far as this, and it is not strange that he had become discouraged, and thought it better to return to the part of the coast where he had found gold. He had had a very hard and stormy voyage, and his ships were becoming more and more worm-eaten, which is something that happens to vessels in these seas if they are not covered with plates of copper. The worms are as large as a finger, and bore through the ship's hull, so that she soon becomes very leaky and unseaworthy.

The last stopping-place eastward was in a little bay, which was so small that Columbus called it El Retrete, or The Closet. In this tiny port the ships were anchored within jumping distance from the shore. There were many alligators here sleeping in the sun. The vessels were so near to land that Columbus could not prevent the rude sailors from getting on shore without permission. They slept in the Indian cabins, an arrangement which soon ended in brawls between white men and natives. The Indians grew more and more fierce and numerous, and Columbus finally fired a cannon, loaded only with powder, hoping to frighten them away. But they answered with hoots and yells, and did not take themselves off until a genuine shot was thrown among them.

After waiting nine days in the little harbor for storms to blow over, the ships set sail again. Columbus turned about and sailed westward from this point, but he was tormented with contrary winds. Presently a nine days' storm arose. The sea seemed to boil, and at night the great waves shone like fire with a phosphorescent light, which must have seemed terrible to the sailors. There was terrific thunder and lightning, and, to add to every other terror, the ships were chased by a great water-spout. The sailors confessed their sins to each other and got ready to die. When the water-spout arose they repeated parts of the Gospel of John, and believed that this was all that saved them from being swallowed up in the column of whirling water.

After a time there came a calm, but the men were gloomy. They shook their heads and did not believe that good weather would last. Many sharks were seen around the ships. This was a bad sign. Sharks, it was thought, could scent the bodies of those who were doomed to die. These sharks were, they thought, waiting to swallow them when the ships should go down. Nevertheless, the men went about fishing for the sharks, using chains for fish-lines and colored cloth for bait. They caught several. Inside of one shark they found a live tortoise, while in another was a shark's head which the men had but just thrown out. In the end the sailors got the better of their fear, and made a meal of the sharks, instead of the sharks making a meal of the sailors. In fact, the provisions were pretty well eaten up by this time. The sea-biscuits that were left were so wormy that the Spaniards preferred to eat them in the dark, for the sake of their appetites.

About the middle of December the ships came to a resting-place in a harbor which looked like a large canal. In this place the Indians built their houses in trees, on poles laid across the branches.

It took Columbus nearly a month to make the distance back to Veragua, where he wanted to go because

BACK TO THE LAND OF GOLD.

it was the place in which he had found gold, and where the Indians all told him there was much of this metal. During all this month the winds were so contrary that Columbus called this region the Coast of Contradictions.

As the mouth of the Veragua River was too shallow for ships to enter, Columbus sailed over a bar and into a river near the Veragua, which he called Belen, or Bethlehem. There were very good signs of gold here. The Spaniards bought twenty plates of the precious metal, some pipes made of gold and pieces of ore. The Indians said that the gold came from the mountains, toward which they pointed, but they said that it was necessary to fast in getting it. The fact is that they had an idea that strict fasting was a kind of charm which gave good luck in finding gold. The Indians of Hispaniola had the same notion.

These Indians brought the white men plenty of fresh fish and ornaments of gold, which they sold for trinkets. They said that the gold came from the Veragua. So Bartholomew Columbus made a trip over to this river. The chief of the river, whose name was Quibian, came down the stream with a number of his men, in canoes, to meet Don Bartholomew. He was a tall, fierce-looking warrior. He gave Bartholomew all the ornaments of gold he had on in exchange for the usual treasures of bells and beads. The chief made Columbus a visit on ship-board the next day. He had a good deal of Indian stolidity, so that the white men could not get much out of him. There was another exchange, however, of trifles for gold ornaments.

After Columbus anchored in the river Belen it

rained for nearly six weeks. During this time the river rapidly swelled, and its swift-rolling currents broke the cables of the ships, almost carrying them away. When the storm at last subsided, Bartholomew Columbus went over to the river Veragua to look for the gold mines the white men had heard so much about. He went up the river until he came to the village of the chief Quibian. This naked monarch, very much painted, came down to the shore to meet the white men. One of his men took a stone out of the river, and, having carefully washed it, offered it to his chief for a seat. The Spaniards imagined that this was a savage style of throne. Quibian and Bartholomew Columbus had a talk, which ended in the chief granting three guides to the Spaniards to take them to the gold mines.

Don Bartholomew left some men to guard his boats, and set out for the mines with the rest of the party. They crossed the windings of a river something like forty times, and slept that night on its banks. The next day they reached the region of gold, and found grains of the precious metal among the roots of the trees. The guides took Bartholomew to the top of a mountain and pointed out the country all around, saying that it was all a country of gold. Bartholomew Columbus might perhaps have seen the Pacific Ocean from the top of this mountain had he been looking for it. The Spaniards afterward heard that the wily Quibian had shown them mines which were in the country of an enemy of his, and that Quibian's mines were really much nearer. They were also told that at these nearer mines a man might gather as much gold in a day as a child could carry.

BACK TO THE LAND OF GOLD. 257

Don Bartholomew took fifty-nine men and went on another expedition westward along the coast, while an armed boat from the ships followed him by water, so that he should not get into trouble. He found many gold plates worn by the Indians, and bought them for trifles. He saw also great fields of Indian corn, and many delicious fruits.

The news of so much gold was enough to inflame the very lively imagination of Columbus. He thought that Veragua must be some part of Asia. It is true that the people were naked and uncouth, but then they might be fishing tribes, while there was possibly some great empire inland. He concluded that the mines of Quibian were indeed the mines of Solomon. He afterward said that he saw more signs of gold while he was in Veragua than he had seen in Hispaniola in four years.

Columbus conceived a plan for founding a new settlement in this land of riches. He decided to leave his brother Bartholomew in command of a colony of eighty men, and hurry away himself for re-enforcements and provisions. All that Columbus could spare now for the colony was a small amount of biscuit, cheese, pulse, wine, oil, and vinegar. But there was food enough in the country—Indian corn, yams, potatoes, bananas, plantains, pine-apples, and cocoa-nuts—while in the rivers there were fish, and for drinks the Indians made a beer of corn and a wine of pine-apple juice. The Spaniards who were to stay began building little houses, framed out of wood and covered with palm-leaves. Columbus made a number of presents to Quibian, hoping in this way to put him in a good humor toward the settlements.

CHAPTER XLV.

DEALINGS WITH QUIBIAN.

1503.

When the admiral tried to sail out of the river he found that since the rains had ceased the water had fallen so low that it was impossible to get over the sand-bar at its mouth. There was nothing to do but to wait for more rain. This was lucky for the little colony, for already there was trouble brewing with the Indians. As Columbus said, "the natives were of a very rough disposition, and the Spaniards very encroaching." The chief, Quibian, presently planned an attack on the white men, hoping to massacre them all and burn their ships.

There was a young man among the Spaniards, named Diego Mendez, who saved the settlement by his shrewdness and courage. He afterward wrote an account of this affair in his will. The Indians seemed to be gathering together. They passed the ships in great numbers. When asked what was going on, they answered that they were going to attack the country of a neighboring chief. Mendez went to Columbus, and said:

"Sir, these people who have passed by in order of battle say that they go to unite themselves with the people of Veragua to attack the people of Cobrava Aurira. I do not believe it; but, on the contrary, I think that they are collected together to burn our ships and kill all of us."

"What are the best means of preventing this?" asked Columbus.

Diego Mendez said that he would go himself and make a visit to the "royal court," as he called the village of Quibian. So he took a boat and rowed along the shore toward the mouth of the Veragua River. He did not go far before he discovered some thousands of Indians assembled on shore. Evidently the "royal court" was on the move. Mendez went ashore, ordering his men to keep the boat afloat at a little distance from shore, so that it should not be captured. He had a talk with Quibian, in which he told him that since he was going to war he had come to go with him. Quibian refused this offer rather too earnestly, and Mendez concluded that his conjecture was right, and that the Indians really meant to attack the white men. So he returned to his boat and lay in sight of the hostile camp all night. This measure disconcerted Quibian very much. Indians always fight by surprises; so Quibian and his men retreated to their village to wait for a more favorable moment. Meantime Mendez returned to Columbus to report. Columbus was anxious to find out clearly what was going on among the Indians; so Mendez offered to go and make another visit to Quibian with only one companion, though this was really a very dangerous undertaking. Mendez and a man named Escobar walked along the beach until they came to the Veragua River. Here they found two canoes with strange Indians in them. These natives told Mendez that the Veragua Indians were planning to attack

19

the white men, that they had given it up because they had been watched, but that they would try it again in two days. Mendez tried to hire these Indians to take him and Escobar up the river in their canoes to Quibian's town. The Indians, however, wished to be excused, and advised the white men to keep away if they did not want to be killed. But Mendez insisted, so the Indians took him and his companion up the river.

The warriors at Quibian's town were all armed and ready for battle. At first they would not let the Spaniards go near the house of their chief. But Mendez told them that he had come to cure this personage of a certain wound that he had in his leg. He made the Indians some presents, and they then suffered him "to proceed to the seat of royalty," as he termed it. This same seat of royalty was situated on the top of a hillock, in the midst of a square which was ornamented by some three hundred ghastly heads of Quibian's enemies killed in battle. Mendez walked boldly through the square straight to the "royal palace." There was a great clamor of women and children, who ran screaming into the palace when Mendez approached. One of the chief's sons came out at this, saying some very angry words in his own tongue. He gave Mendez a push which threw him back a number of steps. Nothing daunted, Mendez showed the fellow some ointment, explaining that he had brought this medicine to cure his father's leg. But the son would not hear to the white man's going in to see Quibian. So Mendez tried another plan. He took out a pair of scissors, a comb, and a looking-glass. To show the Indians the use of these articles, he made Escobar comb his hair and cut it off while he regarded himself in the glass. The natives looked on with interest. When Mendez had been duly barbered, he presented the scissors, comb, and looking-glass to the chief's son. The fellow was appeased, and presently agreed to send for some food. The Spaniards and Indians ate and drank together "in love and good-fellowship, like very good friends," as Mendez said, though he saw nothing of Quibian.

Mendez went back to the ships with his tale. An interpreter whom the admiral had taken from the Indians of the neighborhood also told Columbus that Quibian was indeed planning to massacre the white men. There was no more time to lose. It was a favorite plan of the Spaniards, in managing the Indians, to capture their chiefs. Don Bartholomew now took seventy-four well-armed men with him and quickly ascended the Veragua. When the party reached the village of Quibian, that chief sent them word that they were not to come up to his house. The real reason why Quibian was so jealous of the white men coming to his cabin was said to have been because he was afraid that they would see his wives, for the natives had already had reason to be jealous of the Spaniards with regard to their women. Don Bartholomew paid no heed to the chief's wishes, but walked straight up to the "seat of royalty." He took only five men with him, however, for he did not wish to frighten Quibian into flight. He had agreed with the others that they were to remain below until they heard the report of an arquebuse.

When Bartholomew Columbus got near the chief's house, an Indian came out and begged him not to enter, for the chief would come out to see him. Quibian presently came and sat in his doorway, asking Don Bartholomew to come up to him alone. Bartholomew told his men that they were to stand back until they saw him take hold of the arm of the chief, when they were to come to his aid. He and his Indian interpreter, who was trembling with fear by this time, approached Quibian. Don Bartholomew talked a little with the chief about his wound, and then, pretending that he wanted to look at it, he took hold of the chief's arm. There was a pretty lively struggle between Bartholomew Columbus and Quibian, for they were both powerful men; but four of the Spaniards soon came to the aid of Don Bartholomew, while the fifth fired an arquebuse, which brought the other soldiers rushing up to the "seat of royalty."

DON BARTHOLOMEW EMBRACES THE CHIEF.

Quibian's cabin was surrounded, and some fifty men, women, and children, the most important persons among the Indians, were captured. The warriors wailed aloud, and begged for the liberty of the prisoners, offering to give Don Bartholomew some treasure that they said was hidden in the woods near by. But Bartholomew Columbus was deaf to their prayers. He had found, indeed, some very fine ornaments in the chief's cabin—plates, collars, chains, and coronets made of gold.

The captives were given to a pilot named Juan Sanchez to be taken to the ships. Don Bartholomew warned him not to let the chief escape. Sanchez swore by his beard that nothing of the sort should occur. Quibian was bound hand and foot and tied to a boat-seat. When they got well out into the river the chief made very bitter complaints that the ropes hurt him. Sanchez finally took pity on him, and, unfastening the rope from the boat-seat, held it in his hand. They had nearly reached the mouth of the river, when Quibian suddenly plunged into the water, and Sanchez had to let go of the rope to keep from falling in himself. It was as though a stone had fallen into the river. No more was seen of Quibian, and, as his hands and feet were bound, it was thought that he had been drowned. In spite of this misfortune, Columbus flattered himself that, if he carried off his family and principal men as hostages, there would be peace for the settlement.

When the Spaniards had first come to the river Belen they had prayed for dry weather, and now that it was dry they were praying for rain, that the ships might get over the bar and sail away. Rain came at last, the ships were lightened of their cargoes, and were towed over the bar in calm weather by the boats, one vessel being left behind for the colony. The cargoes were then carried out to them, and they were ready to sail when a favorable wind should come. Riding at anchor outside, Columbus did not know that Quibian was by no means drowned, and was planning to revenge himself on the little colony.

CHAPTER XLVI.

QUIBIAN'S REVENGE.
1503.

QUIBIAN, of course, hated the white men more than ever when he saw his family and friends carried out to sea in the ships. He fell upon the settlement, and this time the Spaniards were taken by surprise. Their first warning was the war-whoop of the savages from the woods close to the settlement. The Indians "began to shoot their arrows and hurl their darts as though they were attacking a bull," as Diego Mendez expressed it. The little palm-leaf houses were soon riddled. Arrows were falling thick as hail, and some Indians ran forward, hoping to club the wounded men in true Indian fashion. Don Bartholomew and Diego Mendez, however, rallied the men, who made good use of their lances and swords, killing such Indians as were bold enough to approach the settlement. The battle lasted for some three hours, but the Indians finally retired, having killed one Spaniard and wounded eight, among whom was Don Bartholomew.

While the fight was going on a boat from the ships came into the river. This boat was in charge of Diego Tristan, who was captain of one of the vessels, and had been sent to get fresh water before sailing. Tristan selfishly refused to land at the settlement for fear so many of the besieged men would try to jump on board his boat as to upset her. When he saw that the fight was over, he went up the river to where the water was fresh, although the men at the settlement had warned him not to go. When he got to a lonely part of the stream where the woods were very thick, he was suddenly attacked by numbers of ambushed Indians, while many canoes shot out from the banks. The panic-stricken Spaniards thought only of shielding themselves from the hail of arrows by their bucklers. Tristan tried to encourage his men to fight, but he was suddenly killed by a javelin entering his eye. Upon this the canoes surrounded the boat, and all the men were soon killed, except one cooper, who fell overboard, dived, and got away by swimming under water. He carried the bad news to the settlement. Presently the bodies of the murdered men floated down the river, and carrion birds could be seen fighting and screaming over them. The colonists were in a panic. The men would gladly have taken the caravel which had been left in the river and sailed out to join Columbus, but the water was again too shallow at the bar. They tried to get out with a boat, but the surf rolled so high that they dared not attempt it.

Meantime the natives were wild with delight over their success in massacring the boat's crew, which was a true Indian exploit. They only waited a good chance to obliterate the settlement. The woods echoed with the blowing of conch-shells and the sound of war-drums, and it was not safe for a Spaniard to venture away from the settlement. They no longer dared to stay in their frail houses which stood near the woods, where the Indians could attack them too readily from behind trees. So they camped on the shore behind a breastwork made of the ships' boats, some chests, and some barrels, with two brass pieces called falconets for artillery.

Meantime Columbus was waiting uneasily on shipboard, wondering why Diego Tristan did not return. The surf was running so high that he dared not risk his last boat; his ships were so rotten and worm-eaten that time was precious if he were to reach Spain, or even Hispaniola; and he was in danger of being struck by a tropical tempest if he stayed much longer on this shore, where he could not put in to harbor. The Indian prisoners, whose captivity Columbus had hoped would secure safety for his colony, were shut up in the hold of the ship. The only opening into this place was a trap-door, which had not been locked at night because several sailors slept about it. Suddenly, in the night, some of the Indians opened the trap-door, and, throwing themselves into the water, made their escape by swimming. When the sleepy sailors were roused to what was going on, they shut the trap-door and chained it down. In the morning, when they entered the hold, they found that the Indians who had not escaped had all hung or strangled themselves, for the decks were so low that the knees of some touched the floor. Such was the despair of these people at the prospect of being carried away from their homes.

Columbus was getting very anxious about the colony. There was a pilot on board, named Ledesma, who thought that if Indians could swim ashore, he could; so he was rowed out to the surf by some sailors, and he plunged in and swam to the settlement. He found the little colony in the misery of a panic, shut up behind a feeble barricade with a small allowance of provisions. Ledesma swam back through the surf to where the boat was waiting for him, and returned to the ships with the bad news of the murder of Tristan and his men and the dangerous predicament of the colonists.

Columbus was in despair. He was anxious about his colony, which it was impossible to succor through the raging surf, and at the same time he feared to waste any more time on this coast with his ships at the point of sinking. Worn out with anxiety and suffering with a fever, he toiled up to the highest part of his ship and wept, while with a quivering voice he cried for help to come to him from Spain. At last he fell asleep exhausted, when he heard in a dream a kind voice reproach him for calling for uncertain help instead of calling upon God, who had given him the keys to the "barriers of the ocean sea which were closed with such mighty chains," and had "brought wonderful renown" to his "name throughout all the land." The voice also remarked somewhat satirically that the acts of God, unlike those of men, answered to his words, and that he performed his promises with interest. "Fear not," the voice said in conclusion; "all these tribulations are recorded on marble, and not without cause."

Not long after Columbus had had this cheering vision, which was no doubt the reflection of his own thoughts and of a spirit rising to fresh emergencies in the face of illness and disappointment, the wind fell and there was a calm, so that the ships were no longer shut off from those on land. Diego Mendez made some bags out of the sails of the caravel that was in the river and put all the sea-biscuit in them. He then fastened two canoes together, and, loading them with the bags of biscuit and ammunition, had them towed out to the ships. By a great deal of hard work all the effects of the colony were moved out in this way, followed by the men, a few at a time, Diego Mendez and five others waiting for the last boat-load.

There was great joy on the ships when the Spaniards had all got safely together again. Columbus embraced the faithful Mendez and kissed him on both cheeks. As there was one ship without a captain, on account of the death of Tristan, Mendez was given the honor, such as it was, of commanding a worm-eaten vessel which was constantly on the point of sinking.

CHAPTER XLVII.

STRANDED.

1503.

Although Columbus was a visionary man when he gave rein to his imagination, he was certainly a very skillful sailor. He started eastward from Veragua, along the coast, instead of sailing north, as his men thought he should do, to reach Hispaniola. They imagined that he was going to undertake the voyage direct to Spain in his leaky ships, instead of going to Hispaniola, and they accordingly grumbled. But Columbus knew perfectly what he was about, and did not wish his men to know, for already some of his old pilots had directed merchant ships to the lands which he had discovered, where they had reaped the profits. He afterward boasted that none of his crew could find the way back to Veragua. The reason why he steered so far east before sailing north was that he wished to allow for the currents, which always carried ships westward in these parts. He sailed eastward to about the region of the Gulf of Darien, and then struck north for Hispaniola.

Columbus had to abandon one of his ships on the way, so worm-eaten was she, and now there were but two left. These were scarcely able to keep above water. The pumps were kept going all the time, and, besides this, the men had to bale constantly with kettles and pans to keep down the water which ran in at the worm-holes. In spite of all the efforts of Columbus to steer far enough east to strike the island of Hispaniola, the currents carried him to the Queen's Garden, off Cuba, instead. Here he anchored, and was struck by a storm, in which three of his cables broke, while the two ships were driven together, smashing the bow of one and the stern of the other. There was only one anchor left to save the admiral's vessel from being driven headlong ashore, and by morning the cable which held the ship to this anchor was worn almost in two.

After the storm was over Columbus bent his course east for Hispaniola. His men were disheartened, his anchors nearly gone, and his vessels "as full of holes as a bee-hive," as he said. He anchored at Cape Cruz, on the island of Cuba, and got a supply of cassava bread from the Indians, for the ships' stores were all used up except a little biscuit, oil, and vinegar. The winds were contrary, the ships were in danger of foundering, and Columbus dared not try to make the remaining distance to Hispaniola. It was necessary to put in to shore before it was too late. So Columbus made a port on the island of Jamaica. As there was no fresh water here, and no Indians from whom he could get food, Columbus sailed eastward to another harbor, which is now called Don Christopher's Cove. Here, on the 24th of June, 1503, the wretched ships were run aground within a bowshot of the shore and fastened together. They soon filled with water up to the decks. Columbus had thatched cabins built on their bows and sterns, and here he resolved to stay for the present. He forbade the sailors going ashore to live, for he knew well what he called the encroaching character of his men, and for the safety of the company it was absolutely necessary that no such troubles should arise between them and the natives as there had been at Veragua. The lives of the Spaniards depended on the friendship of these savage people, for they must starve unless the Indians supplied them with food; while, on the other hand, the natives, once angry, might easily throw a firebrand into the midst of the thatched cabins on the ships—firebrands being favorite weapons with American Indians.

Soon after the white men had stranded on the island of Jamaica the natives began to swarm around the ships, ready to trade. Columbus made it the business of two men to do the trading, so that there should be no disputes. Thus the Spaniards were furnished, for the time, with food. But there were over two hundred hungry men to feed, and the Indians were uncertain and improvident. They did not like to work well enough to raise more food than they wanted. When an Indian had possessed himself of a comb, a knife, some beads, bells, and fish-hooks, in exchange for cassava bread, yams, potatoes, and fruit he was a rich man, and did not trouble himself to bring any more food to the strangers.

When the last ration of wine and biscuit had been dealt out, the good Diego Mendez donned his sword, and with three companions, together with a supply of combs, knives, beads, bells, and a brass helmet in a bag, set out to look for food. He was fortunate enough to find some Indians who were in a good humor and received him very kindly. Mendez made an agreement with these Indians that they were to make cassava bread and hunt and fish for the white men, while they should be paid in blue beads, combs, knives, hawksbells, and fish-hooks. When this agreement had been made, Mendez sent back one of the men he had brought with him to Columbus to tell him of the bargain that had been made, so that he would be ready to pay the Indians when they came with the food. Mendez then went to another village, and made the same agreement with the Indians who lived there. He sent back a second man from here. He journeyed on until he came to the town of a great chief named Huarco. Huarco received Mendez very well, gave

HULL OF A SHIP OF COLUMBUS' TIME.

him plenty to eat, and ordered his people to bring together all the food they could in three days. They brought the food accordingly, and laid it before their chief. Mendez agreed with Huarco that he should keep on sending food to Columbus. He then sent his last companion back to the ships with the provisions. Mendez now begged Huarco to let him have two Indians to go with him to the end of the island, one to carry his food and the other to carry the hammock in which he slept at night. The chief consented, so Mendez traveled alone with two Indians to the east end of Jamaica. Here lived a chief named Ameyro. Mendez and Ameyro struck up such a friendship that they exchanged names, which is a favorite pledge of brotherly love among barbarians. In truth, Mendez wanted to buy a fine, large canoe of Ameyro. He offered him the brass helmet which he had carried with him all the way in a bag, for this very purpose, no doubt. They struck a bargain, with the addition to the brass helmet, of a frock and a shirt, as the price of the boat. Ameyro threw in six Indians to paddle the canoe back to the ships. Mendez reached the vessels with his canoe loaded with a goodly amount of provisions, of which the hungry Spaniards were glad enough, for they were entirely out of food once more; and Columbus embraced the brave Mendez, and gave thanks to God that he had gone safely through so many savage tribes.

CHAPTER XLVIII.

COLUMBUS HAS A PLAN.

1503.

Columbus had been thinking a great deal about how he and his men were to get safely away from this wild island. He wished to get a letter to Ovando, the governor of Hispaniola, so that a ship might be sent to the relief of the stranded crews. The sight of the handsome canoe of Mendez gave him an idea. About ten days after the brave fellow had returned from his foraging trip, Columbus called him aside, and said to him:

"Diego Mendez, my son, not one of those whom I have with me has any idea of the great danger in which we stand except myself and you; for we are but few in number, and these wild Indians are numerous, and very fickle and capricious; and whenever they may take it into their heads to come and burn us in our ships, which we have made into straw-thatched cabins, they may easily do so by setting fire to them on the land side, and so destroy us all. The arrangement that you have made with them for the supply of food, to which they agreed with such good-will, may soon prove disagreeable to them; and it would not be surprising if, on the morrow, they were not to bring us anything at all; in such case, we are not in a position to take it by main force, but shall be compelled to accede to their terms. I have thought of a remedy, if you consider it advisable, which is, that some one should go out in the canoe that you have bought, and make his way in it to Hispaniola, to buy a vessel with which we may escape from the extremely dangerous position in which we now are. Tell me your opinion."

"My lord," answered Mendez, "I distinctly see the danger in which we stand, which is much greater than would be imagined. With respect to the passage from this island to Hispaniola in so small a vessel as a canoe, I look upon it not merely as difficult, but impossible; for I know not who would venture to encounter so terrific a danger as to cross a gulf of forty leagues among islands where the sea is most impetuous and scarcely ever at rest."

But Columbus thought it might be done, and that Mendez was the man to do it.

"My lord," replied Mendez, "I have many times put my life in danger to save yours and the lives of those who are with you, and God has marvelously preserved me. In consequence of this there have not been wanting murmurers, who have said that your lordship intrusts every honorable undertaking to me, while there are others among them who would perform them as well as I. My opinion is that your lordship would do well to summon all the men and lay this business before them, to see if among them all there is one who will volunteer to take it, which I certainly doubt; and if all refuse, I will risk my life in your service, as I have done many times already."

The next day Columbus called all the men together,

and proposed that some one should volunteer for the trip to Hispaniola in a canoe. All were silent. Presently some said that it was an impossible undertaking to cross such a large gulf in a canoe, for ships had been lost in trying it. Then Mendez got up, and said:

"My lord, I have but one life, and I am willing to hazard it in the service of your lordship, and for the welfare of all those who are here with us; for I trust in God that, in consideration of the motive which actuates me, he will give me deliverance, as he has done on many other occasions."

Columbus arose, embraced Diego Mendez, and kissed him on the cheek.

"Well did I know," said he, "that there was no one here but yourself who would dare to undertake this enterprise. I trust in God, our Lord, that you will come out of it victoriously, as you have done in the others which you have undertaken."

The next day Mendez pulled his dug-out canoe up on shore, covered it with pitch, and nailed some boards along the edge to keep out the waves. He then put a mast in her and rigged a sail. Having laid in provisions for his voyage, and taken one Spaniard and six Indians with him for oarsmen, he set out for the east end of Jamaica. Here he met with ill luck, for he was seized by a party of Indians, who resolved to kill him. They had a dispute over who should fall heir to his canoe and its contents, and while they were playing a game of ball to decide this momentous question, Mendez made his escape to the desirable canoe, and so back to the ships, after having been gone fifteen days.

Columbus asked Mendez if he was willing to undertake the voyage again. Mendez said he would, if he might have a force of men to protect him until he could get away from the island. This time a man named Fiesco agreed to go with Mendez, and there were to be two canoes and several other Spaniards, as well as Indian paddlers. Mendez was to carry letters to Ovando, begging for a ship to release the stranded men. He also carried a sad letter which Columbus had written to Ferdinand and Isabella, in which he described his pitiful plight. After taking the letters to Ovando and getting relief for the colony, Mendez was to go on to Spain and deliver this letter to the king and queen. As for Fiesco, if they succeeded in crossing to Hispaniola, he was to return in one of the canoes, so that the stranded men might know that the trip could be made.

Bartholomew Columbus was sent along shore with ninety armed men to protect the expedition. Mendez waited for three days on the end of the island, until the weather was perfectly calm. He then set out. The canoes were provisioned with cassava bread, the flesh of utias, and calabashes of water. Don Bartholomew and his men watched the little crafts until they were mere specks on the water, and then returned to the ships.

CHAPTER XLIX.

A MUTINY.

1504.

The men on the stranded ships kept up hope for a while, looking for the return of Fiesco. But weeks wore by in this dreary business of waiting, and he did not return. Perhaps Mendez and his men had been drowned; may be they had been massacred by Indians after they had reached Hispaniola. Many of the men fell ill of malarial fevers, while Columbus was stretched on his bed, once more, with the gout. Confined to the old hulks, the time hung heavy on the hands of those who were well. They had nothing to do but to imagine evil things. It was very easy for a couple of troublesome brothers named Porras, one of them a captain and the other a notary, to take the lead of the discontents among the common sailors. It was plain, they said, that Columbus was banished from Spain, as well as from Hispaniola. Really, he had sent Mendez and Fiesco to go to Spain and get his recall from banishment, and not to get a ship. As for the admiral, he was content to keep his men here until he was recalled. The proof of all this was that neither Fiesco nor the ship came to their relief. There was nothing for the men to do but to take canoes and go to Hispaniola themselves. Columbus was too gouty; he would never undertake anything of the sort.

A MUTINY.

It was the 2d of January, 1504, about a year from the time that Columbus had landed at Veragua. The ships' crews had already spent four months on the stranded vessels. The mutineers got together, well armed, and burst into the little cabin where Columbus lay ill of the gout. Captain Porras was spokesman.

"How is it, sir," he demanded roughly of the sick admiral, "that you have set your head on remaining here, and do not think of returning to Spain?"

Columbus was astonished at the insolent manner in which Porras spoke, but he answered:

"I have very plausible reasons for staying here in default of all means of transport; and again, I am only waiting for the coming of the ship, which will probably be sent from the island of Hispaniola, to take to the sea and return to Spain—"

"A truce to vain words," interrupted Porras brusquely. "Embark immediately or stay here, in the name of God. As for me, I am going to Spain with all those who will consent to go with me." Immediately there arose shouts from the armed mutineers.

"To Castile! to Castile!" they cried. "Death to him who does not follow! What shall we do, captain?" The whole deck was in an uproar. Columbus jumped out of bed, stumbled and fell from weakness, but got up again and appeared on the deck. Three or four faithful fellows, fearing that he might be hurt by these madmen, took him in their arms and forced him back into his cabin. Don Bartholomew was for attacking the mutineers, lance in hand, but those who were faithful to Columbus persuaded him to go into the cabin with the admiral and leave the matter to them. They then begged Porras to go by all means if he wished to go, saying that nothing was to be gained by violence, since, if he caused the death of Columbus, he would only bring down certain punishment on his own head.

The mutineers proceeded to go. They took possession of ten canoes that Columbus had bought from the Indians, and forty-eight men departed in them as merrily as though they were sure of reaching Spain. The sick men lying on board the ships, seeing so many of the healthy desert them, shed tears. Columbus crept out of his bed to console the poor fellows. He told them that when he got back to Spain he would throw himself at the feet of the queen and beg that they might be rewarded for their loyalty.

Meantime the mutineers took their course to the end of the island, despoiling the Indians by the way, telling them to go to Columbus for their pay, and kill him if he did not pay them well. Arrived at the eastern point of Jamaica, they set out for Hispaniola with Indian oarsmen to paddle their canoes. They had gone four leagues, when the wind rose, the waves ran high, and the brave rebels, beginning to be frightened, turned back for the island. A wave dashed over one of the canoes, and the men began to throw everything out of their boats to lighten them. The canoes still shipped water, and the cowards next threw the Indians overboard, excepting just enough of them to do the paddling. When the poor wretches, exhausted with swimming, caught hold of the canoes, the Spaniards slashed off their hands with swords. The mutineers returned to Jamaica, and ended by roaming about the island and robbing the natives when they dared.

CHAPTER L.

COLUMBUS MAKES USE OF AN ECLIPSE.

1504.

Though the sick on board the ships were left with very few well men to defend them in case of an attack, they really fared better for a while after the mutineers had left them, for there was now more food to be divided among them, and they gradually came back to health once more. But as time went on, the Indians shirked their bargains as usual. They began to hate white men on account of the bad behavior of the mutineers, and when they did bring food they demanded a very large amount of trinkets as pay.

It may be supposed that the stock of beads, bells, fish-hooks, combs, and knives was not endless. Columbus was once more in extremity, when he had a happy thought. He knew that there was to be a total eclipse of the moon in three days. He sent a Hispaniola Indian who was with him to see the chiefs and call a council for the day of the eclipse. When the Indians had come to his council, Columbus made them a speech.

"We believe," said he, "in a God who lives in the skies, who loves the good, and punishes the wicked terribly, even though they are chiefs. You have seen that he did not allow those among us who revolted to go to Hispaniola, while he did let the faithful ones go.

For this reason, this God who loves us, seeing that you will no longer bring us or sell us any provisions, is angry with you, and is going to send you famine and sickness. But as you will not believe these words, he has charged me to let you know that he will show this night a sign of his anger, in throwing a darkness over the moon, which will be a proof to you of the evils with which you are threatened."

The Indians went away when Columbus had done speaking. Some were a little troubled, others laughed.

Evening came. The moon rose, and soon after the eclipse began to come on. It did not take long to rouse the terror of the natives. The darker the moon grew the more frightened they were. They made haste to fill their arms with the first food at hand and run to the ships. They came crying and begging Columbus to intercede with his God, and they would promise that the white men should have enough after this.

Columbus said that he would go and see what he could do. He shut himself up in his cabin, while the Indians stood in terror on the shore as the moon grew more and more dark. Columbus stayed in his cabin during the whole increase of the eclipse. When it was time for the eclipse to begin to diminish, he came out and told the Indians that his God would forgive them if they would treat his people well and give them plenty to eat after this. The Indians were very much relieved when they saw the darkness slowly go off the moon, and they went away thinking, no doubt, that Columbus was a very great medicine-man.

CHAPTER LI.

A VOYAGE IN A CANOE.
1504.

Eight months wore away, and the men on the stranded ships had heard nothing of Mendez and Fiesco. What had become of the adventurers? Could they cross one hundred and eighteen miles of water in canoes? They had started off on a calm evening. There was no wind, and not a cloud was to be seen. In due time the sun rose and beat down on the sea with a terrible heat. Diego Mendez steered, while the Indians paddled. The natives soon became exhausted with the heat, but they would jump into the water, take a swim, and then go at their work again. The red-hot sun went down at last, and by this time the few men in their dug-out canoes were entirely out of sight of land. All night long the Indians took turns in paddling, half of them working while the other half slept as best they could. The Spaniards also slept by turns, for they dared not all sleep at once for fear of treachery on the part of the Indians.

Morning found both Spaniards and Indians worn out. Land was out of sight, and the little canoes stood in great danger of capsizing should the wind come up. The sun rose and began to shine with tropical heat. The improvident Indians had drunk up all their water the day before, and they began to suffer terribly from thirst. The longer the sun beat upon their naked bodies the more they suffered. By noon they were almost fainting, and could not work any longer. At this critical moment Mendez and Fiesco discovered two small kegs of water, which they had probably hidden for such an emergency. They gave this out, a mouthful at a time, to the men, and that mostly to the Indians who did the work.

There is a small guano island called Navaza, which lies some forty miles off Hispaniola. Diego Mendez had steered for this island, hoping to find there water and rest. The Indians paddled feebly on the rest of the day. The Spaniards talked about Navaza, and tried to encourage their men with the thought of soon reaching this resting-place. They calculated that they had come far enough to find it now. They strained their eyes trying to discover the little island, but there was not a cloud nor a speck to be seen on the horizon. And so the sun went down. Now they were afraid they would miss Navaza in the dark, and if this should happen they must all die of thirst and exhaustion before they reached Hispaniola. Some of the Indians lay fainting in the bottom of the boats. One of them died from heat and thirst, and his body was thrown into the water. A few still paddled feebly. The night wore on. The last drops had been drained out of the little kegs. The poor natives tried to cool their mouths with sea-water, which only added to their torment. One by one the disheartened paddlers gave up to suffering and despair, and fell limp in the bottom of the boats. It was late in the night. Mendez had kept up heart till now, but he at last began to despair. The moon was slowly rising, and he was looking hopelessly on, when he suddenly noticed that she seemed to come up from behind something dark. He gave the joyful cry of land. The Indians sprang up, and found that they could manage to paddle a little more. The land was the small island of Navaza, which they would never have found if the moon had not shown it to them in rising behind it.

The canoes sped along now. By daylight the exhausted men landed on the island, which was nothing more than a large rock several miles long. There were no springs here, but the men hurried around and found some pools of rain-water in the hollows of the rocks. They drank it eagerly. The Spaniards warned the Indians against taking too much water, but it was of no use. Several died from overdrinking.

The men next began to think of eating. They gathered some mussels along the shore. Mendez built a fire, over which they broiled the shell-fish, which made a very tolerable meal. Spaniards and Indians rested and dozed all day in the shade of the rocks. When night came they set out once more for Hispaniola, which they could see in the distance from Navaza. They paddled all night long, and the next day they reached Cape Tiburon, in Hispaniola. They landed at the mouth of a beautiful river The Indians were kind to them, and they rested here for two days. It had been agreed that Fiesco was to return to Jamaica and let Columbus know that Mendez had made his trip in safety, but he could find no one who would undertake the terrible journey back with him.

After he had rested, Mendez set out to make the one hundred and thirty leagues to the town of Santo Domingo by coasting in his canoe. After going some eighty leagues he heard that the governor was in Xaragua, engaged in the usual troubles with the Indians. So Mendez walked to Xaragua. According to the story of Mendez, Ovando hanged and burned eighty-four chiefs while he was with him. The Indian princess Anacaona was hanged among other unfortunates for having engaged in a plot against the whites.

In truth, though Columbus had not been a perfect governor, according to the ideas of our day, Ovando seems not to have been a better one. The crowd of adventurers who had come out with him had set off speedily for the region of gold, expecting to pick up a fortune, as people always do in such cases. They trudged to the mines, carrying their stock of provisions on their backs. They dug faithfully, but as they had no skill in mining they found only very good appetites. In a week or two they straggled back to the settlement disappointed men, some of them to die of want, and others to fall victims to the fevers of these sea-coasts.

The Indians had been at first freed from slavery as Queen Isabella had commanded, but Ovando presently wrote to Spain that they would not work unless they were forced, and that they kept away from the white men, so that there was no hope of converting them as the queen wished. The Spaniards on the island were then allowed to force the Indians to work, if they paid them and converted them. This permission soon threw the natives into bondage again, for the pay was almost nothing, and the conversion amounted to a hasty baptism. They were divided up among the white men and made to work for them for six or eight months in the year. They toiled in the fields or in the mines, fed only on a little cassava bread and roots, and scrambling under the table of their masters to get the bones they dropped. When we remember that Indians died off very rapidly in a civilized life at its best, it is not strange that many of these people perished at their work, died on their way home, or after they got to their cabins, when they found them deserted by their wives and children, and nothing planted in their little fields. It is not strange that there were bloody uprisings, which were crushed by the iron heel of the Spaniard, who, dreading the cruel vengeance of barbarians reduced to slavery, was himself made the more cruel by his fears.

Ovando was kind to Diego Mendez, but he delayed about sending relief to Columbus. There were no ships suitable, and there were other reasons for waiting. Really, Ovando feared Columbus, who had been granted, as we know, the government of the lands he should discover so long as he lived, and he much preferred that Columbus should remain in Jamaica for the present.

CHAPTER LII.

A SMALL BATTLE.

1504.

The men on the stranded ships at Jamaica were getting desperate. There was a story that the hull of a vessel had been seen floating in the water, bottom up. No doubt this was the craft sent to rescue them, they thought. Another mutiny had been planned among the men on board the sunken hulks. It was on the point of breaking out, when a sail was seen. There was intense joy among the men. But the ship kept cautiously out to sea, and only a boat approached the old thatched hulls. The captain, a man named Escobar, and an old enemy of Columbus, delivered a barrel of wine and a case of bacon as a present from the governor of Hispaniola, saying that he greatly regretted that he had not a ship large enough to take Columbus and his men over. He offered to take a letter back. Columbus was astonished and hurt at such cool treatment, but he made haste to write a letter to Ovando, and the ship sailed away, leaving the men bitterly disappointed.

It would not do to let discontent breed in the minds of the men, and Columbus pretended to be satisfied with the poor comfort the ship had brought him. He said that he had refused to go in this vessel, since she was not large enough to hold all his company, but that a larger ship would soon come to carry them all away. Really the admiral felt very much injured by the unkind behavior of Ovando and the tantalizing message which he had sent.

Columbus thought that perhaps he might persuade the mutineers to return to duty when they knew that a ship had visited him, that Mendez had really reached Hispaniola, and that there was good hope of relief. So he sent messengers to Porras and his men, offering to pardon them if they would submit. But the mutineers were afraid that Columbus would prevail upon them to give themselves up and then punish them. Some of the men of Porras would have liked to go back to their duty, but Porras talked them down. He told them that no ship had come from Hispaniola. He said that Columbus, who had some mysterious arts, had conjured up the vision of the ship to deceive his men. If there had been a ship, why did it disappear in the night?

Porras even worked his men up to the point of attacking the admiral. Columbus heard that the rebels were coming to attack him, so he sent Don Bartholomew out to meet them with fifty armed men. Seeing that there was likely to be a battle among the white men, the Indians began to gather, very much interested. Don Bartholomew first sent two messengers to Porras to see if he would come to terms, but he would not. Instead of this, he and five of his men made an agreement to try to kill Bartholomew Columbus at all hazards. The mutineers rushed upon the men from the ships. There was a pretty lively skirmish for a little while. Porras struck at Don Bartholomew with his sword, cut through his buckler, and wounded his left hand. But the sword stuck fast in the buckler, and Bartholomew caught hold of Porras, and with the help of others made him a prisoner. Upon this his men fled.

The Indians, as is usual with these savages, were ready to take whichever side should conquer, so they joined the party of Columbus, in great admiration. They examined the three or four mutineers who lay dead on the battle-field, being much interested in the wounds made by the white man's weapons. Among the dead was a man named Ledesma, the same pilot who swam through the surf to get news of the colony at Veragua. He was covered with wounds, and the Indians were examining his corpse, when it suddenly spoke in a deep, hoarse voice. The Indians took to their heels. Did dead men speak among the whites? In reality Ledesma was not dead. He had fallen into a cleft in the rock, and was not found until the next day by the white men. In spite of his many wounds he did not die, but got well; while a man in Don Bartholomew's party died of a single thrust in the leg.

The mutineers soon begged forgiveness. Columbus pardoned them, but let them stay on shore in charge of a captain whom he sent to them, not caring to crowd the ships with troublesome fellows. He kept Porras a prisoner.

A SMALL BATTLE. 291

Meantime Diego Mendez was doing his best for Columbus in Hispaniola. After he had been there eight months some ships arrived from Spain. Mendez purchased one of them, and loaded it with meat, hogs,

MONUMENT TO COLUMBUS AT BARCELONA.

sheep, and fruit, which he bought out of the money that belonged to Columbus from the profits of the gold mines at Hispaniola. The man who was an agent for Columbus to collect his share of the profits took command of the ship, while Mendez went on to Spain. By this time Ovando was getting ashamed of the way in which he had treated the great discoverer; for people in Hispaniola began to talk about it, and priests even preached about it from the pulpit.

Eight days after the rebels had surrendered to Columbus the ship from Hispaniola came. Great was the joy of Columbus and his men. They had lived a year, wanting but a few days, on their stranded hulls, in danger of Indians and starvation. They bade good-by to the old thatched vessels with light hearts, and sailed for Hispaniola, friends and enemies together. The winds and currents were so contrary that it took them more than a month to reach the settlement at Santo Domingo, so persistently did misfortune follow them.

CHAPTER LIII.

THE LAST DAYS OF COLUMBUS.
1504-1506.

Columbus spent about a month on the island of Hispaniola. He caused the ship he had come in from Jamaica, and one other vessel, to be fitted up for a voyage to Spain. Some of the men who had been in Jamaica with him chose to stay at Hispaniola. Columbus spent all the money he could collect from his revenue to take himself and the rest of his company home. The return voyage was very stormy. The mast of the ship that the admiral sailed in was carried away. He was forced to get into the other vessel with his brother, son, and servants, and send the dismantled one back to Hispaniola. The weather continued to be very bad, and the mast on the second vessel was sprung in four places. Columbus was lying in his bed with an attack of the gout, but he told his men what to do. They shortened the mast, and tied pieces of wood taken from the cabins to the weak places. Suffering very much from his painful illness, the admiral landed at last in Spain, and was carried to Seville, where he hoped to rest and get well again.

When Columbus reached Spain Queen Isabella was on her death-bed. She had tried to befriend Columbus to the last. She reproved Ovando when she heard that he made trouble about the collecting of what was due to Columbus, and censured him for not admitting the discoverer to harbor on his voyage out, as well as for not heeding his warnings about the storm. She had been very indignant when she heard of the execution of Anacaona, and had made King Ferdinand promise that he would remove Ovando.

The exposure that Columbus had undergone on his voyages, his anxieties, and the painful disease from which he suffered, had undermined the constitution of the great explorer. Soon after he reached Seville, as he was too ill to travel on horseback he asked for a litter from the chapter of the cathedral to go to court in. The canons lent him the litter which had been used for the funeral of Cardinal Mendoza, though it was not the custom to do such a thing. But Columbus heard of the death of the queen, and knew that the court would be in trouble and confusion, and as the weather was cold and stormy, and he very ill, he decided not to go. He had friends at court who were doing their best in his cause—his son Diego, the faithful Mendez, and others.

Columbus lay on his bed of pain all winter, longing for news or writing melancholy letters to his friends at court. Sometimes he wrote words of advice to his eldest son, as though he did not expect to live long. He wished Diego to be especially kind to Ferdinand, to conduct himself toward him as an elder brother should. "Ten brothers would not be too many for you," he wrote. "In good or bad fortune, I have never found better friends than my brothers."

The death of Queen Isabella was a great loss to

Columbus, for she had been a good friend to him. The king was much more selfish and calculating than the queen. Ovando had succeeded in making Hispaniola profitable, while Columbus had not, so that the king was slow in keeping his promise about removing the governor. The discoverer suffered from delays in getting his dues paid him from his share of the gold found in Hispaniola, but he was more anxious about the titles and honors which belonged to him and his descendants. It was his ambition to found a great family. His sons had been brought up at court, and he wished to leave them grandees.

King Ferdinand, on the other hand, found it very inconvenient to be limited to the family of Columbus in selecting a governor for Hispaniola, and he wished the admiral to take some estates and titles in Spain, in place of the revenues and honors that had been granted to him in the New World. But the great discoverer, though he was suffering extremely, never for a moment relaxed his determination to defend the rights which he had earned by the discovery of a new world.

As the winter wore away Columbus determined to attempt the journey to court, in hopes of bringing matters to a decision by his presence. There was a law then in Spain which forbade people to ride on mules, because mules had been used so much for riding that the breed of horses had declined. Columbus sent to the king and asked permission to use a mule in going to court, since the mule was a more quiet animal, and would not rack his gouty frame as would a horse. A royal ordinance was issued in February permitting Columbus to ride a mule, but it was not before May that he was well enough to go to court even in this way. The court was at Segovia when Columbus journeyed painfully there, and he followed it afterward to Salamanca and Valladolid. The king received Columbus with kindness, but continually put off granting him his rights, hoping that he finally would make up his mind to become a Spanish nobleman, and be satisfied with that.

The winter of 1505-1506 was the last winter of the great man's life. He began to despair of living to enjoy his rights should he regain them, and he begged the king to give the government of Hispaniola to his son Diego. "This is a matter," he said, "which touches upon my honor. As for all the rest, do as your Majesty thinks proper; give or withhold, as may be most to your interest, and I shall be content. I believe it is the anxiety caused by the delay of this affair which is the principal cause of my ill-health." But it was all of no use. The king replied favorably, but delayed.

King Ferdinand was not really king over Castile, but the kingdom went to Isabella's heirs. As Queen Juana of Flanders was her eldest daughter, she and her husband, Philip the Handsome, were to govern Castile. These monarchs arrived in Spain in the last months of the life of Columbus. King Ferdinand and his court went to meet them, but the discoverer was past following in the train of a court. He sent Don Bartholomew to see the young king and queen and beg for justice at their hands.

Columbus grew more and more ill at Valladolid. The old wound which he had received at some time in his youth reopened. He made his will and got ready to die. He bequeathed to his descendants the revenues and rights that he hoped would some time be restored to his heirs, for he had nothing else to give. "Hitherto," he says, "I neither have had nor have I now any positive income." He made Diego his heir, and after him his descendants. In case the line of

HOUSE IN VALLADOLID IN WHICH COLUMBUS DIED.

Diego failed, Ferdinand and his descendants were to succeed to the estates and honors. Diego was to relieve all poor relatives. One of the wishes of Columbus was that a chapel should be built in the beautiful Vega Real, where masses should be said for his soul and the souls of his family. Another place toward which his affections turned was his native city of Genoa. He wished one line of his descendants to be maintained in Genoa. And, finally, he did not forget his project for the rescue of the Holy Sepulchre.

Having settled his affairs, Columbus took the sacraments of the Church, and, surrounded by seven faithful servants and his two sons, he died on the twenty-first day of May, 1506. In the excitement over the arrival of the new king and queen, the death of the great discoverer passed unnoticed, except by the few who loved him.

The body of Christopher Columbus was probably interred in Valladolid, until several years after his death, when it was removed to the vault of the Carthusians, in the convent of Las Cuevas, at Seville. The remains of his brother Bartholomew and of his son Diego were afterward laid beside those of the great admiral. The three bodies were later removed to the cathedral in Santo Domingo. In 1795, when Santo Domingo fell into the hands of the French, the Duke of Veragua, a descendant of Columbus, removed what was thought to be the remains of his famous ancestor to Havana, Cuba; but as there had been no record kept of the exact burial-place of Christopher Columbus, it is a disputed question to-day whether the dust of the great admiral rests in Santo Domingo or in Cuba.

It was some years before Diego Columbus, the eldest son of the discoverer, could get any recognition of the rights which his father had bequeathed him from King Ferdinand, who was again governing Castile as regent, his daughter having become insane. Diego once asked King Ferdinand "why his Majesty would not grant him, as a favor, that which was his right, and why he was afraid to confide in the fidelity of one who had been reared in his house." The king

CATHEDRAL AT SANTO DOMINGO, WHERE COLUMBUS' REMAINS WERE BURIED.

answered that he could trust him, but that he did not like to repose so great a trust at a venture in his children and successors.

"It is contrary to reason and justice," said the young man, "to make me suffer for the sins of my children and successors, who may never be born."

Diego Columbus finally got permission from the king to go to law to get his rights. A great lawsuit followed, which was decided in favor of Diego. Nevertheless, the young man would scarcely have got any of his rights had he not married a young lady named Donna Maria de Toledo, a niece of the Duke of Alba and a relative of Ferdinand himself. With the influence of a powerful Spanish family to help him, Diego Columbus was finally made governor of Hispaniola, though this was only a part of the privileges to which his father had an undoubted right, and it was not until some years later that he was allowed the title of viceroy.

In 1509 the son of Columbus sailed for Hispaniola with his young wife, his two uncles, Bartholomew and Diego, and a fine retinue in which were many young ladies of good blood and no fortune, who went out hoping to find husbands among the rich planters of Hispaniola. Don Diego and his wife held a little court more splendid than any that had been seen in the New World before, and built a beautiful mansion to live in.

Diego, however, succeeded to some of his father's troubles as well as to his honors. There were the inevitable revolts and squabbles, for which the governor had to bear the blame and travel to Spain to answer the consequences. Among other things, there was a tedious suit to recover revenues to which the descendants of Christopher Columbus were entitled, in the great profits which poured in from the New World. It was on one of his journeys to Spain, in 1526, when he was pushing this suit, that Diego Columbus, following the court of Charles V, grandson of Ferdinand and Isabella, fell ill of a fever. He tried still to follow the movements of the court in a litter, and died, as his father had done, away from home and a solicitor at the Spanish court, leaving his affairs still unsettled. The management of them now fell to his wife, the vice-queen, and she tried to push the suit for the benefit of her little son Luis; but there was finally a compromise, and the heirs of Columbus accepted a pension and the dukedom of Veragua, in place of the honors which Columbus had hoped to leave to his family. The descendants of Columbus still live in Spain and succeed to the title of Duke of Veragua.

The little Ferdinand, who was with Columbus on his last and most dangerous and irksome voyage, became a great book collector. Like all the relatives of Columbus in Spain, he was finally enriched by the court out of the revenues of the New World and with gifts of Indian slaves. He collected a very fine library, and built a sumptuous mansion, which stood in the middle of a beautiful garden filled with trees brought from the New World.

Christopher Columbus died still holding many mistaken ideas about the lands he had discovered. He thought Cuba part of the main-land, and he still believed the main-land, to be some outlying part of Asia, while the more civilized lands, he imagined, might be reached by a strait leading into some inner sea, like the Mediterranean in Europe. But in spite of his mistakes in geography, Columbus knew perfectly that he had made a very great discovery and earned for himself a glorious name.

It was the fashion early in the century, when Washington Irving wrote his famous Life of Columbus, to see no faults of character in the great discoverer, and to represent him as little less than a hero or a saint. Indeed, one biography of the discoverer was written to persuade the Catholic Church to canonize him. There has been a natural reaction from such an attitude of over-reverence, and to-day scholars are inclined to take an opposite view, some even going so far as to represent the famous discoverer as rather worse than an ordinary sinner. Both views of the character of Columbus are no doubt extreme. He was the product of his age—an age of new-born discovery, of greed for wealth, of bigotry, and of

PALACE AT SANTO DOMINGO BUILT BY DIEGO COLUMBUS.

ruthlessness. He outran his age in a lively belief in the possibility of passing around the globe, while he was not above the spirit of his time when he accepted a pension for first seeing land, a reward which he might have turned over to a common sailor. He made great discoveries, but he held mistaken ideas about them—notions which he once childishly tried to enforce by the oaths of his men. He had expected and promised great riches, and he planted the evil of Indian slavery to force this expected wealth from the bowels of the earth; while his whole after-life became a bondage to the necessity for verifying his rash promises. If his colony was the home of misfortune, it is no more than can be said of all early plantings in America and of all newly discovered gold regions. His unchecked imagination carried him on many flights—flights which some writers think to be mental wanderings, since they contrast very unfavorably with his reasonable project, as it seems to us, of attaining the East by sailing westward. He was a modern man in his discovery of a new hemisphere, he was a child of the middle ages in his fancy for turning the profits of his voyages toward a crusade to rescue the Holy Sepulchre. But whatever were the faults of Columbus, it must still be admitted that he was a very great man, in that he gave himself to a great purpose which he carried out in the face of immense obstacles, while he bore with no little fortitude a life of great hardship and a career of thwarting misfortune.

THE END.

D. APPLETON & CO.'S PUBLICATIONS.

APPLETONS' CYCLOPÆDIA OF AMERICAN BIOGRAPHY. Complete in six volumes, royal 8vo, containing about 800 pages each. With sixty-one fine steel portraits and some two thousand smaller vignette portraits and views of birthplaces, residences, statues, etc.

APPLETONS' CYCLOPÆDIA OF AMERICAN BIOGRAPHY, edited by General JAMES GRANT WILSON, President of the New York Genealogical and Biographical Society, and Professor JOHN FISKE, formerly of Harvard University, assisted by over two hundred special contributors, contains a biographical sketch of every person eminent in American civil and military history, in law and politics, in divinity, in literature and art, in science and in invention. Its plan embraces all the countries of North and South America, and includes distinguished persons born abroad, but related to American history. As events are always connected with persons, it affords a complete compendium of American history in every branch of human achievement. An exhaustive topical and analytical Index enables the reader to follow the history of any subject with great readiness.

"It is the most complete volume that exists on the subject. The tone and guiding spirit of the book are certainly very fair, and show a mind bent on a discriminate, just, and proper treatment of its subject."—*From the* Hon. GEORGE BANCROFT.

"The portraits are remarkably good. To any one interested in American history or literature, the Cyclopædia will be indispensable."—*From the* Hon. JAMES RUSSELL LOWELL.

"The selection of names seems to be liberal and just. The portraits, so far as I can judge, are faithful, and the biographies trustworthy."—*From* NOAH PORTER, D. D., LL. D., *ex-President of Yale College.*

"A most valuable and interesting work."—*From the* Hon. WM. E. GLADSTONE.

"I have examined it with great interest and great gratification. It is a noble work, and does enviable credit to its editors and publishers."—*From the* Hon. ROBERT C. WINTHROP.

"I have carefully examined 'Appletons' Cyclopædia of American Biography,' and do not hesitate to commend it to favor. It is admirably adapted to use in the family and the schools, and is so cheap as to come within the reach of all classes of readers and students."—*From* J. B. FORAKER, *ex-Governor of Ohio.*

"This book of American biography has come to me with a most unusual charm. It sets before us the faces of great Americans, both men and women, and gives us a perspective view of their lives. Where so many noble and great have lived and wrought, one is encouraged to believe the soil from which they sprang, the air they breathed, and the sky over their heads, to be the best this world affords, and one says, 'Thank God, I also am an American!' We have many books of biography, but I have seen none so ample, so clear-cut, and breathing so strongly the best spirit of our native land. No young man or woman can fail to find among these ample pages some model worthy of imitation."—*From* FRANCES E. WILLARD, *President N. W. C. T. U.*

"I congratulate you on the beauty of the volume, and the thoroughness of the work."—*From the* Rev. PHILLIPS BROOKS, D. D.

"Every day's use of this admirable work confirms me in regard to its comprehensiveness and accuracy."—*From* CHARLES DUDLEY WARNER.

Price, per volume, cloth or buckram, $5.00; sheep, $6.00; half calf or half morocco, $7.00. Sold only by subscription. Descriptive circular, with specimen pages, sent on application. Agents wanted for districts not yet assigned.

New York: D. APPLETON & CO., 1, 3, & 5 Bond Street.

D. APPLETON & CO.'S PUBLICATIONS.

COLONIAL COURT-HOUSE, PHILADELPHIA, 1707.

"This work marks an epoch in the history-writing of this country."—*St. Louis Post-Dispatch.*

THE HOUSEHOLD HISTORY OF THE UNITED STATES AND ITS PEOPLE.

For Young Americans. By Edward Eggleston. Richly illustrated with 350 Drawings, 75 Maps, etc. Square 8vo. Cloth, $2.50.

FROM THE PREFACE.

The present work is meant, in the first instance, for the young—not alone for boys and girls, but for young men and women who have yet to make themselves familiar with the more important features of their country's history. By a book for the young is meant one in which the author studies to make his statements clear and explicit, in which curious and picturesque details are inserted, and in which the writer does not neglect such anecdotes as lend the charm of a human and personal interest to the broader facts of the nation's story. That history is often tiresome to the young is not so much the fault of history as of a false method of writing by which one contrives to relate events without sympathy or imagination, without narrative connection or animation. The attempt to master vague and general records of kiln-dried facts is certain to beget in the ordinary reader a repulsion from the study of history—one of the very most important of all studies for its widening influence on general culture.

"Fills a decided gap which has existed for the past twenty years in American historical literature. The work is admirably planned and executed, and will at once take its place as a standard record of the life, growth, and development of the nation. It is profusely and beautifully illustrated."—*Boston Transcript.*

INDIAN'S TRAP.

"The book in its new dress makes a much finer appearance than before, and will be welcomed by older readers as gladly as its predecessor was greeted by girls and boys. The lavish use the publishers have made of colored plates, woodcuts, and photographic reproductions, gives an unwonted piquancy to the printed page, catching the eye as surely as the text engages the mind."—*New York Critic.*

GENERAL PUTNAM.

"The author writes history as a story. It can never be less than that. The book will enlist the interest of young people, enlighten their understanding, and by the glow of its statements fix the great events of the country firmly in the mind."—*San Francisco Bulletin.*

New York: D. APPLETON & CO., 1, 3, & 5 Bond Street.

www.ingramcontent.com/pod-product-compliance
Lightning Source LLC
Chambersburg PA
CBHW030008240426
43672CB00007B/870